P9-CEX-753

Small Miracles
for Women

Also by these authors:

Small Miracles
Small Miracles II
Small Miracles of Love & Friendship

Small Miracles
for Women

Extraordinary Coincidences of
Heart and Spirit

Yitta Halberstam
&
Judith Leventhal

ADAMS MEDIA CORPORATION
Holbrook, Massachusetts

Copyright ©2000 by Yitta Halberstam Mandelbaum and
Judith Frankel Leventhal. All rights reserved. This book, or parts
thereof, may not be reproduced in any form without permission from
the publisher; exceptions are made for brief excerpts used in
published reviews.

Published by Adams Media Corporation
260 Center Street, Holbrook, MA 02343
www.adamsmedia.com

ISBN: 1-58062-370-0

Printed in Canada.

First Edition
J I H G F E D C B

Library of Congress Cataloging-in-Publication Data
available from the publisher.

Cover photo by Barbara Peacock/FPG International LLC.

This book is available at quantity discounts for bulk purchases.
For information, call 1-800-872-5627.

Visit the Adams Media home page at http://www.adamsmedia.com.
Visit the *Small Miracles* home page at
http://www.adamsmedia.com/smallmiracles.

For my mother, Claire Halberstam,
and my mother-in-law, Sima Mandelbaum,
two women who broke the mold.
—Y.H.M.

For my mother, Rose Frankel,
my mother-in-law, Anne Leventhal,
and my aunt, Margaret Handler,
who all embody strength and nurturing love.
—J.F.L.

Introduction

Our thanks go first and foremost to YOU, our cherished readers, whose enthusiasm for the message of our books has been boundless and immensely gratifying. Because of YOUR warm response to our previous books, we are thrilled to have been able to write this fourth book in the *Small Miracles* series. We have been enormously moved by your kind and sincere letters and are very heartened to know that *Small Miracles* has brought you joy and comfort. You are the co-creators of our books, and we applaud YOU for your open hearts and contagious excitement. Thank you!

Over the years, we have been struck by the generous response of *women* to the message of our books. But it really shouldn't surprise us: Women always seem to be in tune with the messages sent to us through the miracle of coincidences. We know that we tend to live more in our hearts than in our heads, and we filter reality through the prism of Spirit rather than through the five senses that men typically favor. Some would argue that women are more intuitive, more open to life's mysteries, more mystically inclined, and we would certainly agree.

Despite our ever-demanding schedules, and crazy, harried lives, women especially need to take time to stop and see the magic of the tiniest moments. These are *Small Miracles*, and we dedicate this book to you.

This collection celebrates the milestones and markers of every woman's life: birth, love, marriage, friendship, and beyond. We have searched the country to find true stories that would speak to women of all ages and of all faiths. Quite simply, *Small Miracles for Women* addresses our shared experiences—the triumphs and the defeats, the celebrations and the losses sustained during a lifetime. And woven throughout these stories is the magic, the sense of awe, the understanding that these experiences are being orchestrated by a loving hand that gently guides and connects us all.

Do women live *too* deeply? Being conscious, being awake, being open is part of the divine experience, part of feeling integrated into the cosmic order. So we say, you can never live deeply enough! We hope that *Small Miracles* will continue to open doors into that deeper, more profound experience and be a corridor to the mindfulness that makes life that much more sweet. For in a world where chaos and a sense of existential meaninglessness often swirl around us, possessing the knowledge that we are part of a divine plan and have sacred purpose is infinitely comforting.

In this new millennium, may we all continue to be blessed with *Small Miracles*—both large and small—and with the wisdom to recognize them when they touch our lives.

—*Yitta Halberstam and Judith Leventhal*
June, 2000

*T*he pain hit with sudden fury.
No, thought Monica Droddy.
I can't be having this baby now. Not here in the car!

Frantically, she looked around. The country road was dark and deserted. No house beckoned, no phone booth appeared. Outside, icy winds pounded the car. It was almost midnight, New Year's Eve, 1998, and she was all alone. The pain lashed so hard she couldn't hit the brake.

How had it come to this? Only two days ago, her doctor had smiled reassuringly. "Everything looks fine, Monica. The baby should be here mid-February." Confident she wouldn't deliver for six weeks, Monica had decided to make the hour's drive to her parents' house in Maryland and surprise them for New Year's Eve. Now here she was, on the outskirts of her hometown, screaming with terror as she felt the baby coming right in the car.

Just go to the hospital. It's only 10 minutes away, she told herself. But it was no use. She could feel the baby about to appear. *Oh God, please don't let it come just yet; it's going to suffocate. . . . Please God. . . .* Fighting back hysteria, she took off her shoes so she could pull down her pants. She was now near her old high school. As she desperately tried to figure out how to drive and deliver the baby at the same time, she noticed a neighborhood she'd never seen before. She turned into it and found herself on a little cul-de-sac. Somehow, she maneuvered the car to a stop and stumbled out into the freezing night.

Four houses, all with lights on, faced her. *Grandma,* Monica prayed. *You can see from heaven. Help me. Where should I go?*

Without thinking, without understanding why, Monica ran past the three houses that were closest. Staggering with excruciating pain, shivering in her stocking feet, feeling the baby coming any second, Monica chose the house that was farthest away.

"Help me!" she screamed, pounding on the door. "I'm having a baby! Call 911!"

No one answered. *Don't make me deliver my baby all by myself on this porch, God. . . . Help me, please. . . .*

"Don't let her in." A man was speaking on the other side of the door. "There's a crazy lady out there."

Now a woman's voice answered, softly but firmly. "I'm opening the door anyway," she said.

The door swung open. An elderly woman in a bathrobe waved Monica inside. "Don't worry," she said kindly. "My daughter is here."

In the upstairs bedroom of her parents' house, Dianne Minter slept, oblivious to the pandemonium below. That morning in Virginia, the snow had been falling so hard that she had almost decided to cancel her visit to her parents. But by early afternoon, the snow had let up enough for her to risk the four-hour drive to Maryland. The trip had been exhausting, and Dianne had fallen asleep at ten o'clock, too tired to join her parents as they rang in the New Year.

Now her mother's voice roused her from her sleep: "Dianne! Come quick!" And another woman's voice, hysterical: "Oh God help me! My baby's coming!"

Dianne raced out of bed to the top of the stairs. She looked down at the screaming stranger. Then she flew into action. "Mom, call 911! Dad, get sheets!" she barked as she ran down the stairs.

"Everything's going to be okay," she said, taking Monica's hand. "I'm a nurse. I worked labor and delivery for four years. Let's get you upstairs onto a bed."

At the top of the stairs, Monica stopped. "It's coming now!" she screamed. Dianne laid her down and prepared to deliver the baby.

"What position did your last ultrasound show?" Dianne asked.

"Breech. Is it going to be okay?" sobbed Monica.

"Yes, of course. Just try not to push, and keep breathing."

But despite her reassuring words to Monica, Dianne felt sick with panic. The baby was preterm and in breech position. And she had no equipment. How could she possibly deliver this baby alive?

Calm down, Dianne, she told herself. *God did not send this woman to you for this baby to die. Just do what you have to do and everything will be fine.*

"Monica, I see it coming!" Dianne said. "Don't push!"

At that moment, the doorbell rang and a volunteer emergency worker bounded inside. He was only 18 years old, nervous and unsure of what to do.

"Get the emergency oxygen and the delivery kit—now!" Dianne ordered.

He ran back to the ambulance and returned just as the baby was born into Dianne's waiting hands.

"Congratulations, Monica. You have a boy."

"I don't hear him! Why isn't he crying?" Monica screamed.

Without answering, Dianne unwrapped the cord that was strangling his tiny neck. She suctioned the mucus from his nose with the emergency kit, cut the cord, and stimulated him till he cried.

"Give me oxygen! Quick! He's turning blue!"

As soon as she stabilized his color, Dianne gently placed the baby on Monica.

By now the paramedics had arrived, ready to take Monica to the hospital. "Hold him next to your skin. Your body temperature will help protect him," Dianne said, placing layer upon layer of cloth on top of the baby. "Good luck!" she called as the paramedics carried Monica and her newborn outside into the 15-degree night.

The next day, Dianne walked into Monica's hospital room, carrying flowers. "These are for you," she said, placing them on the windowsill. "And this is for the baby." As she leaned in to hand Monica a teddy bear, she broke into a startled laugh. "Hey! You've got my dad's pillow!"

"How did that happen?" Monica said. "Should I give it back?"

"Keep it. It will bring you luck."

"You brought me luck, Dianne. Without you . . . my beautiful baby . . . my Jacob . . . would be . . ." Unable to say the word, Monica burst into tears and threw her arms around Dianne's neck. The two women held each other close and cried together.

At last Dianne said, "It wasn't me who brought you luck, Monica. This was meant to be."

"It was a miracle," sobbed Monica.

"There's something I want to ask you," Dianne said. "This morning we went out and locked your car. And we saw where you parked it. There were three houses closer than ours. So why on earth did you choose us?"

"I really don't know. I remember I prayed to my grandmother to help me. And then without thinking, I ran to your house. That doesn't make sense, does it? I was in my stocking feet, and I was in so much pain that your house seemed a hundred miles away. I don't know. I just chose you."

— *Peggy Sarlin*

*T*he glitter of green stones drew me to the display case. The light bounced off silver and glass. Amid the throng of holiday shoppers, I stood in the corner area reserved for fine jewelry and gazed at the bracelet, noticing its unique handiwork. The beaten silver, fashioned to resemble diamond chips, was exquisite, and it was encrusted with dozens of dark green emeralds. I knew this was a one-of-a-kind treasure.

As I admired the intricate piece, I remembered a promise my husband had made. David had bought me a lovely gift on our honeymoon four years earlier. He had selected an emerald-green Austrian crystal and seed-pearl bracelet in honor of my May birthstone. As he fastened it on my wrist, he lovingly said, "I promise you that I will buy you real emeralds someday soon. Just wait." I loved the sentiment of his honeymoon gift, but deep down I excitedly looked forward to the fulfillment of David's promise.

Until that time, however, I still loved wearing my crystal bracelet. I wore it frequently, each time fondly remembering the island boutique where we had found it. Whenever David saw the bracelet, he would smile and reassure me that the time was coming soon when he would keep his promise.

It became our habit over the years to look in every jewelry store window. David's pursuit became symbolic of his devotion to me, and I loved him for it. We wandered in and out of countless shops, becoming somewhat discouraged when we realized that the cost of his promise was well beyond our means. I started to doubt that I would ever own what David desired to give me. David, however, never lost his faith.

On the day I found the particular bracelet, we were in the mall during the last week before Christmas to buy gifts for our children. Finances were tight and we had agreed there would be no exchange of gifts between us. We had just completed one of the most stressful years of our marriage. With David's diagnosis of Huntington's disease, our lives had forever changed. This fatal neurological disorder had pitched us into a panic, not to mention near bankruptcy.

I looked up into David's eyes and saw love shining even brighter than the green stones. I could tell what was in his mind. Nothing short of this bracelet would satisfy his original honeymoon promise. But I knew there was no way we could possibly afford it. I tried to tell him, but the words died on my lips. He'd had so many disappointments that year; I didn't have the heart to tell him that we absolutely shouldn't consider it.

Thinking fast, I came up with a reason to refuse the offer I knew I couldn't accept. I have large wrists and normally bracelets don't fit. As the store clerk reverently lifted the object out of the case, I knew it would be too small. The silver and green made a colorful contrast against my brown skin. I silently acknowledged how much I wanted the bracelet while still hoping it would not fit. As the clerk reached around my wrist and closed the intricate clasp, my heart both leaped and then quickly plummeted. It fit! It was perfect. Yet I knew it would be wrong to buy it. The unpaid bills, with more looming in the future, had placed a vise around our checkbook.

I glanced at my husband, my best friend, and saw him beam. This gentle man was now the victim of a very cruel disease. His was a sentence with only one verdict: untimely, slow, and cruel death. My eyes brimmed with tears as I realized we would not live out our dream of growing old together. The jewelry before me was meaningless compared with the hope of living a lifetime with this man. But to David, the bracelet on my wrist would not be just one more bauble in a crowded jewelry box. Rather, this was his love for me displayed for all the world to see. To David, a promise made was a promise to be kept. I sadly realized that he might not have many more months or years in which to keep his promise. Suddenly it became the most important covenant ever made, and I knew that somehow I had to juggle the bills to let him have the honor of keeping it.

"Do you like it?" he whispered. Hearing the hope in his voice, mingled with the adoration in his eyes, was heart-wrenching. It was clear that David cherished me. All he had ever wanted, from the day we met, was to make me happy. I was a lucky woman, indeed.

I heard myself saying, "Yes, honey, I love it. It's exactly what I want."

The clerk reached out to remove the bracelet. I could not believe this little object had worked its way into my heart so quickly.

"How much is it?" I finally asked.

Slowly the man turned over the little white tag.

Two hundred and fifty dollars. Surely this was a mistake! I had seen enough fine jewelry to know that price was only a fraction of its worth.

The man began to extol the beauty of the item, pointing out the 180 emeralds in a handmade Brazilian setting. But even though $250 was an incredible value, it might as well have been $2,500, given our meager budget.

Without thinking, I asked, "Would you take $225, tax included?"

I was amazed to hear myself ask the question, because shops in malls do not normally bargain.

The clerk looked at me in surprise, but answered, "That will be fine."

Before he could change his mind, I whipped out my credit card, watching David beam with pride. The man quickly handled the transaction and we were on our way. Every few steps we would stop and look at the bracelet. Before we reached the car, David said: "When I get sicker and eventually am no longer with you, I hope you'll look at each emerald on the bracelet. Every one will remind you of something special we've done: a trip we took, a movie we saw together, or a moment we shared. This will be your memory bracelet."

I began to cry. David's concern was not for his own failing health, but for my welfare after he was gone.

As we worked our way home in rush-hour Honolulu traffic, I wondered just how we would pay for the bracelet. Oddly enough, however, I never really panicked. I was somehow only curious about how it would all work out. We talked as we drove, and every so often we looked admiringly at the miracle of the promise kept.

Upon arriving home, I grabbed the mail and began to open it as we walked inside. Among the usual bills were two cards. One was from a church where I had sung several times that year. It was a thank-you note for my music ministry, along with a gift—a check for $200. I was speechless. I reached for the second card and slit it open. Out fell two bills: a twenty and a five. My benefactor preferred to remain anonymous. The card was simply signed, "Anonymous."

I looked up at David and we both shook our heads in amazement and then began to laugh. Even as I had inexplicably felt the urge to negotiate our price in the mall, the payment of David's promise was already in our mailbox. God had already taken care of every detail, right down to the penny.

The bracelet is just a piece of jewelry, something I could have lived without. But the memories represented by each emerald have helped make me the person I am today.

The exquisite joy of our relationship and the unspeakable grief of dealing with David's disease have allowed me to develop in ways I never could have anticipated. I have thought about God's promise to each of us—that he will be with us every step of the way in life, if we will just ask him.

Just as God has never stopped believing in me, David never stopped believing in his bracelet promise. Each time I wear my emeralds, I count the memories tucked away in my heart, and I feel new courage as I think about David's faith and God's promises.

—*Carmen Leal-Pock*

ᘓᘐ᙭᙮

Comment
Not only does God send us exactly what we need, sometimes He even mails it a day early!

I found them in the attic while rummaging through a trunk. Several years before, I had tucked away vintage samplers that I had gathered from antique shops and garage sales. Now I spread them out with pleasure, reading the sayings that exhorted the virtues of patience, patriotism, work, and life's simple joys. As I scanned my collection, I envisioned a doting grandmother hovering over her granddaughter, teaching her skills for life— reading, arithmetic, and the needle arts.

Stepping back into the past for a few minutes was just what I needed. For days I had been feeling frustrated. I hadn't been able to do anything to cheer up my coworker Cathy, and it was on my mind. As we worked together at the hospital, Cathy had talked about caring for her terminally ill mother, and I could see the sadness in her eyes. It made my heart heavy: Why couldn't I think of any way to help Cathy?

I looked at my array of samplers. My small collection spanned more than a century, and each work was as personal as a fingerprint. I knew that samplers had been used in colonial times as educational tools, and the folk and religious wisdom they imparted had been part of a young woman's upbringing. As years passed, samplers had served more decorative purposes; some were sparked with whimsy, and others had a charm that clearly reflected the personality of the seamstress.

I unearthed a box of dusty old picture frames and matched the samplers to the appropriate size, shape, and design, envisioning just the place to hang them in a downstairs hallway. The next morning I carried my box of nostalgia to the local framing shop, eagerly awaiting the results.

A week later I picked up the framed samplers. As I turned to leave the shop, the owner stopped me. "A businessman visiting from a nearby city happened to be in here the other day and noticed one of your samplers," she told me. "He said his mother is seriously ill, and that the verse reminded him of her. He wondered if you would be willing to sell it."

I gazed at the one she was pointing to:

Mother's love
is like a fragrant rose
with sweetness in every fold

I remembered when a lady at a flea market had told me to dab lemon juice and salt on the old stained linen and place it in the sun. The refurbished beauty was one of my favorites, and I had no intention of parting with it. But to be polite, I jotted down the businessman's name — William Eads — and his phone number.

The next day as I surveyed my treasures, my eye fell on this message:

*It is in loving
not in being loved
the heart is blessed.*

How loving was I being if I didn't at least speak to
William Eads? Somewhat reluctantly, I dialed his
number several times that evening, but got no answer.
I've done my part, I reassured myself in relief. Now I'll
get to work in peace. I planned and measured for my
arrangement, then carefully drove the nails into the wall.

But as I raised the "Mother" sampler, I found I was
unable to lower it to its position on the nail. I gazed
again at the fragile cross-stitching of threads forming the
complete picture. For a moment it seemed the stitches
almost came alive with the vitality of the fingers that had
lovingly made them, fingers whose activity conveyed a
sense of commitment, shared an honest sentiment. . . .

Maybe this sampler was meant to be shared.

The next morning, before I left for work, I dialed the
number again. William Eads answered. "You don't know
who I am," I explained, "but the owner of the framing
shop told me your mother is very ill. . . ."

He knew immediately who I was. "Would it be
possible to buy that sampler from you?" he asked. "It
reminds me so much of my mother. She adores samplers.
She used to work on them herself until she became too
sick." He paused and took a breath. "And her love—just
as the sampler says—is like a rose."

Suddenly, I was flooded with thoughts of the sweet-smelling climbing roses my own mother once tended. "I want to give it to you," I blurted out. "Tell me your address and I'll mail it."

"I can't tell you how much I appreciate this," the man said excitedly. "But you don't need to mail it. I'll be visiting my mother this weekend, and she lives close to you. Would you mind leaving the sampler at her house?"

He gave me directions to his mother's home. I quickly wrapped the sampler in a brown paper sack and dashed off to deliver it before heading to work.

I pulled up in front of a brick split-level home. When I rang the bell, a middle-aged lady came to the door. She explained that Mrs. Eads was unable to leave her bed. I introduced myself and handed her the package. "It's from Mrs. Eads's son," I said, eagerly handing her my parcel. It suddenly felt wonderful to have given something I loved to a perfect stranger.

Later that day I spotted my friend Cathy walking across the hospital grounds. When I greeted her, she gave me a smile more cheerful than I had seen in weeks. "So what sort of strange men were you telephoning earlier today?" she asked playfully.

I looked at her in astonishment. How did she know what I had been doing?

"Does the name William Eads ring a bell?" Cathy asked. I nodded.

"He's my brother," she said. "Eads was my maiden name. And you just delivered that sampler to my mother. My brother called and told me about your visit and your gift." Cathy explained how touched her mother had been when she saw the sampler that had meant so much to William. "I can't wait to see it," she said.

For a moment I stood staring at her; then I broke into a beaming smile of my own.

Warm friendship
like the setting sun shines
kindly light on everyone

Little stitches, little gestures. Stitch after stitch, hand over hand. And so it goes, over the years, in gestures of caring and love.

How do you make a sampler yours for keeps? By feeling its message in your heart and sharing that message with others.

—*Roberta Messner*

*S*he was only 19 years old, but she was wise beyond her years. And she knew enough about life to know that the love she had found at such a young age was pure, good, and enduring.

We are soul mates, she often thought, kindred spirits. *How blessed I am to have David in my life and for such a long time, too.*

Their respective mothers—who were good friends— often laughed that their children were destined-to-be from the time they were toddlers. When the women had first met in Warsaw, the two little ones on their laps had made funny faces at each other and then shared a lollipop. Afterwards, they cried as they parted.

David and Miriam went to school together, and their friendship blossomed into love. In high school, they were already a pair. Their mothers rejoiced to see the melding of their families this way, but privately wondered if young love could last. It did.

David presented Miriam with a tiny diamond engagement ring on her 19th birthday. "I will always love you," he said.

"You are my destined one," she replied.

But destiny had other things in store for them. Hitler's soldiers marched into Warsaw one day, and life as they had known it ceased to exist.

Miriam caught a glimpse of David at the train station, where the Jews of her neighborhood were being herded into cattle cars. For resettlement, they were told. Chaos reigned as crowds jostled, children wailed, soldiers barked orders, mothers cried. But when Miriam saw David boarding one of the cars at the other end of the platform, her heart lurched and time stood still.

"David!" she screamed. "David!"

She dropped her bags and dashed across the platform.

"Miriam!" her mother cried in alarm. "Don't leave me, please!"

"Where do you think you're going?" a soldier said as he blocked her path. "Get back to your line!"

"Please . . . ," she begged him. "My fiancé . . . I just saw him . . . I need to talk to him . . . please . . . just for a minute. . . ."

"Get back in line," the Nazi hissed. "Now!"

The "resettlement" story was, of course, a lie. The train led them to Auschwitz, where Miriam's mother was selected for the gas chambers. Young and still healthy, Miriam was allowed to live, though barely.

Not a day passed that she didn't look for David. When she passed the men's barracks, when a detail of men passed her, she always inspected their ranks yearningly. Her eyes roved ceaselessly. All she asked for was a glimpse of his face. But she didn't know if he was interned at Auschwitz. She didn't even know if he was alive.

She kept on asking everyone she encountered whether they had seen David in Auschwitz or had met him in any of the other camps they had been transferred from, but no one had any news. She refused to believe that he was dead. In her prayers, she begged God to keep him safe. Take me instead of him, she cried.

At the war's end, Auschwitz was liberated, and Miriam was among the skeletal survivors. Her compatriots, after slowly recovering in DP (displaced persons) camps, made their way to new homes in Israel, America, Canada, South America, Australia—but not Miriam. She stayed behind in Europe for more than three years to hunt for David. But he had vanished, and people told her that after three years it was time to give up. "You have to begin life anew," they urged. "Just like us."

How can I live life without David? she wondered. Life has no meaning without him.

There were those who felt compassionate towards her and those who felt impatient. "Time to move on," they exhorted. "Most people never have that kind of love in their life to begin with. Be grateful you had it at all, even if it was just for a brief time."

Finally, Miriam began to feel the futility of her quest. In a DP camp in Sweden, she met Saul, a kind, gentle man with whom she could make a life. She didn't love him; but she liked him well enough. She was honest about her feelings, and he accepted the limitations. Many survivors didn't want to wait for love; they wanted to rebuild their shattered lives as quickly as possible. Camaraderie and companionship were sufficient for them. Their needs were humble; they didn't ask for more.

So they married in Sweden, but made plans to emigrate soon. Miriam's entire family had been wiped out, so she felt unattached to any particular place. She assumed, however, that, like most survivors, they would move to Israel or to the United States. When her husband told her he had an excellent opportunity in Port Elizabeth, South Africa, she was taken aback.

"Port Elizabeth?" she asked in dismay. "I never heard of it. Why do you want to go there?"

"A friend of mine — someone who lived in my town before the war — has moved there and established a thriving business. He needs help and would welcome me into his company as a partner. I don't have such an opportunity anywhere else."

"But . . . I thought we would move to a large Jewish community . . . in the United States . . . in Canada. . . . Even Johannesburg would be better. What kind of place is Port Elizabeth?"

"It's a small coastal city, and it does have only a tiny Jewish population," her husband conceded. "But it's the place where I've been offered an opportunity."

Miriam was reluctant and unhappy. She had had visions of relocating to a vibrant, heavily populated Jewish city where the sheer numbers of coreligionists would make rebuilding easier. She was not so sure what kind of life she could make in Port Elizabeth. She felt like a leaf blown off a tree, driven hither and thither, with no control over its destiny.

"So we'll go to Port Elizabeth," she finally shrugged in resignation. "After everything we've been through, what difference does it make?"

It was at a Jewish agency in Port Elizabeth, where she had gone to fill out some papers for German reparations, that she first saw him.

He was bent low over the clipboard, scribbling furiously, but she recognized the nape of his neck, the contour of his head, the color of his hair. She swore she could smell him across the reception room; she inhaled it as one would an aromatic scent.

"David!" she screamed. "David!"

He looked at her and their eyes locked. His face turned white.

"Miriam! My God, Miriam! You are alive?! Oh, my God, I was told that you were dead!"

"Me, too. I heard you were dead. I hunted for you for three years," she cried.

"I searched for you for two," he said. Then he dropped his eyes to the floor.

"Miriam," he said anguished, "there are things I would say to you, would like to say, but cannot anymore. . . . Miriam, I am married."

"David," she said softly, "you don't have to explain anything to me. I understand . . . you thought I was dead; I was in the same position. I am married, also."

He looked at her sadly. "Miriam . . . what shall we do? It's not as if we are in London or Sydney or even Johannesburg. The Jewish community in Port Elizabeth is very small; our paths will cross often."

"David, we must do the honorable thing. We cannot hurt or humiliate our spouses in any way. I don't think we should tell them about our encounter today, nor the history of our involvement. Why inflict unnecessary pain on them? It would probably cause them tremendous discomfort to know about our past and to know we were living in this same city together. . . . And," she went on with greater conviction, "we must not speak to each other ever again; we cannot. It would be too painful for us, and dangerous."

"But Miriam!" he protested. "Not to talk to you . . . ever! That's too harsh; it's crazy; it's unacceptable."

"David," she said firmly, "I love you very much. I will never love anyone as I love you. But this is what we must do in order to protect the sanctity of our marriages."

For 40 years, they lived in the same community in Port Elizabeth — bearing children, raising families, marking milestones — without acknowledging one another's presence ever again. They honored their vows, protected their spouses' dignity, and tried to live life as fully as they could, knowing that the love of their life was leading a parallel existence only a few short blocks away.

Every now and then, in the synagogue, at a wedding, in the local food market, they would encounter one another briefly, and their eyes would flicker longingly at each other. A quick, imperceptible nod was the only greeting that acknowledged the encounter. A dewy, misty look would always appear in Miriam's eyes after one of these encounters, and her heart would ache. She never shared her pain with anyone, and the two would have gone to their graves with the secret, had an extraordinary turn of events not taken place.

After 40 years of marriage, Miriam's husband Saul died suddenly one day of a heart attack. And just two months after Saul's death, David's wife was felled by a fatal stroke.

For a full year after their respective spouse's deaths, the two made no attempt to contact each other. But each had heard the news about the other.

They mourned their spouses, with whom they had fashioned good and decent lives, and their grief was deep and sincere. But as they marked the year of mourning, they also listened for news of one another.

After the first yahrzeit (anniversary of death) of each spouse had been commemorated, David picked up the phone.

"Miriam?" he said.

At their wedding a few weeks later, Miriam and David finally revealed to their children and close friends the secret they had kept for so many years. They explained how torturous it had been to live in such a small community and see each other constantly; how wrenching it had been—a trial from God. All this time they had never stopped loving each other, but their commitment to their spouses had never wavered either. Forty years later, they were finally able to fulfill the love that the war had aborted.

ぐ℮℀℮℮

Comment

Love borne in compassionate silence arouses the help of Heaven.

*S*he had avoided this moment for years, knowing that once she spoke those magic words, her life would never be the same. Now the moment was here. Slowly she rose to her feet, her chair loudly scraping against the basement floor. Thirty faces turned to look at her. She took a deep breath and dared herself to plunge ahead. "My name is Ella* and I'm an alcoholic," she said.

The knowing sympathy she saw in other people's eyes gave her the courage to continue. "I've got to stop drinking. Because it's not just me I'm hurting anymore. I've got a baby now. My Henry . . ." She stopped, overcome by a sudden vision of Henry, smiling and reaching out his chubby little hands to her. "He . . . he's . . . so beautiful . . . I would die rather than hurt him. Because I know what it's like to be hurt. My father was a drunk and I'll do anything to keep Henry from feeling the pain that my father caused me."

After the meeting, Ella sat quietly, slumped over in despair. She would never be able to get sober. And even if by some miracle she did, how could she possibly stay sober, day after day, year after year? The meeting had been filled with stories of terrifying struggles, of constant temptations, tragic losses, and hard-fought victories

---

* Names followed by an asterisk are pseudonyms.

rendered hollow by a sudden, sickening fall from grace. The battle for sobriety never ended, no matter how safe you thought you were. Even with her love for Henry to guide her, how could she win?

"Ella?" She looked up. A pleasant-looking young woman put her hand on her shoulder and gave it a gentle squeeze. "Don't worry. I can tell you're in it for the long haul."

The long haul . . . Many times over the next two years, those words echoed in Ella's mind. Faithfully every day, sometimes twice a day, she attended a support group meeting, gradually finding the strength to give up drink. Sometimes at a meeting she would see Lauren, the pleasant-looking woman, who was battling a deeply ingrained drinking habit. According to the group's rules, everyone kept personal details to a minimum and didn't socialize outside of meetings. But even within these restrictions, Ella began to think of Lauren as her friend. She had such an uncanny knack of saying to Ella exactly what she needed to hear, of finding the perfect words to give her comfort and confidence.

Once, when Ella was panicking about getting through the night, Lauren had nodded gravely. "For you, Ella, it's 18 minutes at a time." Eighteen minutes at a time! She could probably handle that. And if she could get through 18 minutes, followed by another 18 and another, maybe she could get through the long haul after all.

Another time, Ella talked about her father and the rage she felt toward him. She described how he drank away his frustrations as a painter, his mood growing blacker and more dangerous with every sip. Lauren responded by speaking movingly about her own creative struggles and how for years she had found inspiration in a bottle. "You don't know how much courage it takes to be in the arts. Isn't there any part of you that can begin to forgive your father?"

Begin to forgive . . . As she tucked Henry in at night, those words resonated. She loved Henry with all her soul, yet she was hardly a perfect mother. Who knows? Maybe someday Henry would have to forgive her. . . . And with that insight, for the first time, Ella felt her heart softening towards her father.

Sometimes Lauren didn't even need words to help Ella. Once Ella was walking down the street in the throes of craving a drink. Every bar she passed seemed to call her inside. I'll never make it home, she thought. I'm just not strong enough. As she felt herself giving way, she noticed a pleasant-looking woman walking towards her. It was Lauren. She smiled and gave her a little nod and walked on—but that was enough. Ella turned from the bar door and headed home.

After two years of hard-won sobriety, Ella finally felt strong enough to take the next step in her recovery— making amends to everyone she had ever wronged. The process was painful, but strangely exhilarating, too. As

Ella sorted through her mental file of people she had mistreated, the image of Sofia deeply troubled her. At her next meeting, she stood up and spoke. "I grew up mostly abroad," Ella said. "My father left this country to paint, and he took us with him. And I was really raised by this wonderful peasant woman—Sofia, our housekeeper. My own parents were chaotic and crazy, but Sofia was very calm and kind. She gave me structure and rules that made sense. And I think that any sense of discipline that I've been able to find in myself these last two years to get sober, I owe to her.

"And I feel so bad because every Christmas, she writes and begs me to visit. And I never pay any attention to it. She retired and moved back to her little village and I think she's lonely. And now I realize, she was like a mother to me. And if she wants me to visit, I should honor her by doing it. But I can't . . . I just can't. Because I'm so afraid." She paused, then caught Lauren's eye and gathered the resolve to continue.

"I'm just so scared that I won't find any meetings there. The only way I keep sober is by going to a meeting every single day. And they don't have support groups over there like we do here. And if I can't find one, I'll fall right back into the pit and wake up dead drunk and hate myself forever."

"Ella," said Lauren, "do you really think it's important that you go?"

"Yes."

"Then why don't you go?" said Lauren. "Just trust that if you need something badly enough, you'll get it."

Lauren's words convinced her. Ella made arrangements for Henry to stay with her sister, and she flew to Athens, Greece, her childhood home. As soon as she landed, she began searching for a support group meeting. To her amazement, she found one right away, located in the very church where she had been confirmed. The meeting wasn't until evening, and as Ella wandered the city, she became increasingly agitated. So many memories . . . At lunch, the waiter poured a glass of wine without asking, and she almost drank it before she convinced him to take it away. By the time she entered the church for the meeting, she felt very frail and vulnerable. Her footsteps echoed off the marble floor as she slowly, self-consciously made her way to a seat. A dozen ravaged-looking old men turned to stare at her. She was the only woman there. Ella took her seat, aching with loneliness. Another set of footsteps echoed in the church. Ella turned to look — and there was Lauren.

"No!" Ella gasped. "It can't be!"

Lauren stared at her, eyes widening in shock. Then the two women fell into each other's arms.

"What are you doing here?" said Ella.

"Giving a concert. And going crazy trying not to drink!"

"I'm going crazy too!"

"Well, let's go crazy not drinking together."

That night, Ella couldn't sleep. She stared at the ceiling, marveling at the extraordinary coincidence that had brought Lauren and her together, thousands of miles from home. Was it mere chance, just a meaningless random event? Or was somebody upstairs working miracles on her behalf? Maybe she wasn't alone in her fight to stay sober. Maybe—was it possible?—she had magic on her side.

Over the next few days in Athens, Ella and Lauren helped each other stay the course. But as Ella's departure date loomed, she began to panic. The time had come to visit Sofia. That meant spending two weeks in a tiny, remote, unsophisticated mountain village. Forget about magic and miracles and anything else she'd been imagining. She would never, ever find a support group there.

"What'll I do?" she wailed to Lauren. "I've never gone a single day without a meeting."

"Remember what I told you," Lauren said gently. "Just trust that if you really need something badly enough, you'll get it."

With Lauren's words to comfort her, as always, Ella set out on her journey. She arrived at Sofia's doorstep, tired and anxious, still brooding about finding a meeting. Sofia rushed out and smothered her with kisses. "Come in, come in! I'm so happy you're here!"

Nervously, Ella followed Sofia inside. The first thing she noticed was a door on the right. Attached to the door was a golden plaque, inscribed with the prayer of her support group.

"Sofia! Why do you have this here?" she exclaimed.

"Oh, that . . . The priest knows I have an empty room in my house, and he asked if he could use it for a kind of meeting that is called AA. Every night, people come to this room. Don't worry. They won't bother you."

"I'm not worried, believe me!" Ella threw her arms around Sofia, laughing. "Not worried at all. In fact, I think I'll join their meeting!"

Today, Ella is a confident young woman who has been sober for more than 10 years. "When I look back at that trip," she says, "I can see it was the turning point. So much magic happened to me that I finally started to learn how to trust. Sometimes you need proof that you really will get what you need. That trip was my proof."

—*Peggy Sarlin*

Comment

Miracles often arrive at the moment we depart from fear and head toward faith.

"*If* I ever get remarried, all I want is a bridal shower!"

This was the one and only wish of my dear mother-in-law, who had been divorced for eight years. It must have been poignant for her to attend the bridal showers of her two son's brides—my sister-in-law and myself—in a solitarily single state. My heart ached for my mother-in-law when I heard her wonder out loud: "Will I ever have the opportunity to be as happy as my children?"

After marrying off two wonderful sons (one of which is my husband) within the same year, my mother-in-law must have figured that three weddings is the charm. She finally met Mr. Right, and we all rejoiced for her. I also remembered the wistful request she had made so many months before, and I felt determined to fulfill it and throw her an unforgettable shower.

I went to work right away on arrangements. There were invitations to mail, chairs to rent, a house to clean, food to cook. This was going to be the party to surpass all parties . . . and a surprise one, to boot. I wanted to make sure that every single detail would be perfect. To add some "class" to this special event, I borrowed party favors, accessories, and decorations from a friend of mine who was a professional party planner. As I left her home, my arms laden with bride-and-groom dolls, colored glasses, and wooden bird cages to decorate the table, my generous-spirited friend called after me: "Wait! There's one more thing I want to lend you."

It was her most prized possession—an antique oversized crystal champagne glass. The perfect centerpiece!

"I know how much this party means to you," she said, "so I really want it to be special. Please take this—but please remember to be extra careful with it. It's my favorite piece, and I was never able to find another one anywhere."

"You're a doll," I said gratefully. "What a friend! Don't worry; I'll guard it with my life."

I rushed home, thrilled to have such professional-looking accoutrements to dress up my party table. I couldn't contain my excitement for long, so I decided to set the table then and there—several days in advance of the party! When I finished, I stood back from the table and admired my handiwork. I called my husband into the dining room and got the kudos I had hoped to elicit. The table did indeed look very festive.

Soon, different family members (except for my mother-in-law, of course!) trooped in for a tour of the much-touted table. "She's going to love it," my grandmother enthused, "especially that champagne glass. What a fabulous piece! She is going to be so surprised."

Two days before the bridal shower, however, that "surprise" was almost aborted when I got an unexpected call from my mother-in-law's fiancé. He and my mother-in-law were two minutes away by car, he said, and wanted to stop by and give my husband some old mail. Oh, no! I groaned inwardly. In a panic, I rushed to the dining room, swept everything off the table, and quickly crammed drawers and cabinets with the party stuff. As the doorbell rang, I reached for the last thing on the table — the champagne glass — and carefully put in on the floor of our walk-in storage closet. By the time I answered the door, not a single piece of "evidence" remained to testify to the big surprise that I was planning for that Sunday. My mother-in-law and her fiancé stayed for several hours, so I could not reset the table until the next morning.

I rushed around the dining room, pulling objects from their hiding places, duplicating my movements of the previous day, and all was going well until it was time to place the finishing touch on the table: the antique champagne glass. As I opened the storage closet to retrieve the glass, my heart sank when I saw it on the floor . . . broken. My heart began to pound and my face flushed in shame. *This is my favorite piece!* I could hear my friend saying. My own staunch reassurance — *Don't worry; I'll guard it with my life!* — came back to haunt me, in mockery. How could this have happened?

My father was the blameless culprit. He had opened the closet door earlier that morning in search of the vacuum cleaner and had accidentally stepped on the glass.

I tried to squelch the panic rising up in me, but I was utterly devastated by what had happened. Every single member of my extended family was enlisted to scour all of Manhattan's department and specialty stores (no mean feat) in search of a replica. But my friend had been quite correct in her assertion to me that she had never been able to find another one. Despite everyone's best attempts, the champagne glass couldn't be found anywhere.

"Don't worry," my husband said as he tried to calm me. "God will reward you for being so kind to my mother—he will surely pay you back."

He was trying valiantly to alleviate my distress—which I appreciated, of course—but I could hardly believe that there was any way this awful scenario could improve.

I put my worries on the back burner when Sunday came, the day of the shower. My mother-in-law was genuinely surprised, quipping that she felt like a kid all over again, as she eagerly opened her gifts with excitement and joy.

Cookbooks . . . pots . . . linens . . . everything a new bride needs and loves. I had never seen her happier. By all counts and everyone's standards, the bridal shower was a huge success. The antique champagne glass wasn't missed by anyone except myself.

When the guests started to leave, the family members and friends who had graciously stayed behind to help began to fold the chairs and clear the table. It was then that a friend of my mother's, whom I did not even remember putting on the guest list, approached me and said, "I have a gift for you."

"For me?" I asked, confused. "You mean for my mother-in-law, right?"

"No, for you," she said. "I never attend a party without bringing a gift for the hostess." She handed me a gift-wrapped box, congratulated my mother-in-law once more, and left.

Later, when the house became quieter and most of the guests had left, I opened the box. Inside was an exact twin of the antique champagne glass!

I checked the invitation list. This woman's name was not on it.

"Things like this don't happen in real life," I said to my husband, who had tears in his eyes himself.

"God really does reward us in mysterious ways," he answered. "You did something very special for my mother and really made her feel good. In turn, God sent this woman to you to replace the broken glass. One good deed begets another!"

— *C. Stern*

❧

Comment
The only gift that can never be replaced is the gift of love.

*O*ne morning in 1975 in Greenwood, South Carolina, Dorothy Nicholas sat scribbling at her kitchen table. She was trying to compose an appropriate slogan. Even though Dorothy is an award-winning writer and former advertising copywriter, she sometimes has trouble finding just the right words. And she sensed that these needed to be perfect.

The words were for a sign hanging over the self-service gas station Dorothy managed with help from her disabled husband, Fred. They had started working a week ago, pulling their trailer from Orlando up to Greenwood, and the job seemed simple enough, just sitting at a drive-up window, taking money from customers.

"It was a bit of a lark," Dorothy admits. "Fred and I called a lot of places 'home' during those years, because we both yearned to travel, and with our children grown, we could do it." Sometimes they settled for a while and took jobs, and this was one of those times.

There was already a lighted advertising sign on top of the building, but Dorothy's new boss had told her she could replace the message with anything she liked. "I had heard that this chain of stations was frequently robbed," Dorothy says, "so I was thinking about a safety-related slogan." At the same time, she felt that God was nudging her, encouraging her to make her trust in Him known to others. She tried several ideas; then inspiration struck.

"What do you think of this?" she asked Fred.

He studied her scrawl: GOD IS OUR SECURITY GUARD—ALWAYS ON THE JOB. "That says it pretty well," he told her. The next day, he spelled it out on the lighted board.

The sign was impressive, but it seemed to have little or no effect on anyone. Few customers commented on it.

After five months, the wanderlust struck again, and Dorothy and Fred resigned and took off in the trailer. Time passed.

"Sometimes we would travel that route, going from Florida to North Carolina, and I always felt a little glow as we'd drive by the sign," Dorothy says. Subsequent managers had liked it well enough to keep it up. But, remembering her strange urgency to find just the right words, Dorothy wondered if the sign had really mattered to God, after all.

In 1988, Dorothy and Fred found themselves in Gainesville, Florida. At church they met Janet* and Larry,* a young couple living nearby. The four got along well, and when Dorothy and Fred had some temporary health problems, their new friends proved to be a blessing, running errands, providing an occasional meal, and just being there. "I don't know what we would have done without you," Dorothy told Larry more than once. She was growing quite fond of this kind, clean-cut young man.

One evening Dorothy invited Janet and Larry over for dinner. The four sat around the table, talking in a leisurely way. Fred and Dorothy were surprised to hear that Larry had grown up in Greenwood.

"Why, we worked there once . . . ," Dorothy began. Had they ever met Larry? She started to ask him, but having begun to talk about himself, Larry couldn't stop.

"I've had a pretty rough past," he went on, pent-up words suddenly tumbling out. At 16, he'd gotten involved with the wrong crowd and had spent a year in reform school. After his release, he'd wanted to start over again, but because of his record, he couldn't find a job.

"One night in 1975," Larry continued, "I decided to rob a gas station for money to leave home." There was a self-service station nearby, so he stole his father's gun and car, and just before closing time, he drove up to rob the woman sitting at the window.

But before pulling his gun, he glanced at the roof of the building. There had always been a sign there, but someone had recently changed the words. "When I read the message," Larry said, "I knew I couldn't rob that place—or do anything else illegal." He went home, prayed all night, and begged God to help him straighten out his life.

Dorothy and Fred looked at each other. "What did the sign say, Larry?" she asked gently.

"I've never forgotten those words," the young man assured her. It said, 'GOD IS OUR SECURITY

.' And he is,
that night, and he

13 years, but now
nging, the need to
sed her small act
s side.

Joan Wester Anderson

The right word in the right place at the right time . . .
Through this, worlds are created and lives rebuilt.

First came the volley of shots, then the high-pitched screams, and finally, the irrevocable silence of death. Later, in the women's barracks, hushed whispers would tell of an aborted escape by some of the men. And much later, a young woman by the name of Esther would learn that Yidel—her beloved brother and only surviving family member—had been among the casualties.

Now her world was totally broken, destroyed. She was the last, the remnant. Two years earlier, when Hitler's nightmare had first been unleashed in Poland, her beloved parents had been shot down by the Nazis in cold blood, and Yidel—older by four years—had become both father and mother to her. Yidel had been her sanctuary and port, her stalwart companion during her sojourn through the camps. Now he was gone. She was 20 years old and completely alone.

"He died a hero," she tried to console herself. "And better a bullet in the back than death in the gas chambers." That ignoble death would soon be *her* fate, she was sure, when she discovered that the next stop on her journey was the infamous death camp Sobibor.

Until now, Esther had been relatively fortunate. Over the course of the past two years, she had been moved from camp to camp, but all of them had been "work" camps, where slave labor was harnessed for the Third Reich, where it was still possible to survive.

But Sobibor, like Treblinka and Belzec, was a "death camp." Its only industry was extermination. When Esther was told she would be transported to Sobibor, she knew the end was near. Sobibor existed for one purpose only—the manufacture of death.

Strangely, though, when she entered the main gate of Sobibor together with the crush of hundreds, it was a sense of elation, not despair, that suddenly engulfed her. *You are going to escape from here!* a voice deep inside her exulted. That certainty surged through her even as her eyes absorbed the impossibly high barbed wire fence, the formidable watchtowers that loomed overhead, the menacing guard dogs with bared teeth.

Her first minutes at the death camp served only to confirm her incongruous conviction that here at last, in the jaws of hell, she was going to be blessed. For whenever a new transport arrived, a selection was made. Almost all of the arrivals were sent immediately to the furnaces, but during each selection a handful were plucked out from the crowd and spared.

Sobibor was not only a death factory, but also the place where Nazi personnel lived, and skilled laborers were required to tend to their needs and maintain the camp. Sometimes the call came for carpenters, or goldsmiths, or dentists; sometimes musicians, or singers, or dancers were recruited to entertain the Nazis when they were bored at night. On this particular day, the

Nazi recruiter just happened to be looking for women who knew how to knit, a skill at which Esther excelled.

Out of the transport of 800 young people who arrived at Sobibor that day, only seven were selected for a temporary reprieve. And Esther was one of them.

"Eventually, they'll replace us with others," one inmate murmured to another.

"No one leaves here alive."

"We must escape!"

And so, almost as soon as she had arrived at the camp where her fate never looked bleaker and the odds never seemed greater, Esther joined with other feisty spirits to plot the famous Sobibor uprising—the biggest prisoner escape of World War II.

On the eve of the revolt, Esther bade farewell to those in the barracks who would not be joining their effort to escape. They were either too sick or dispirited to try. *We're never going to make it, either,* Esther thought sadly as she kissed her friends good-bye. But better a bullet in the back than death in the gas chambers.

That night her sleep was restless and her dreams had a hallucinatory quality to them. In one of those dreams, she saw her deceased mother enter the main gate of Sobibor.

"Mama," she cried out in disbelief. "What are you doing here? Don't you know that we're going to escape tomorrow?"

"I know," her mother answered calmly. "That's why I came."

"Ester'le," her mother said tenderly, "I am here to tell you that you will escape! And this is where you must go when you do."

Her mother took her by the hand, led her out of the gate, and brought her to a barn. They went inside the barn, and there her mother pointed toward the loft and said in a clear, firm voice: "Here you'll go and here you'll survive."

And then she disappeared.

Esther awoke with a start and, trembling, roused the woman who shared her bunk. Shaking, she recounted the dream, but Esther's friend was unimpressed and made short shrift of its import.

"Listen," she scoffed, "you're nervous, you're scared, of course you would dream about the escape. But the dream doesn't mean anything. Don't take it seriously."

Esther was unswayed by her friend's dismissive words.

"Nonetheless," she vowed, "if somehow I miraculously survive, I won't rest until I find the place my mother showed me!"

In the dream, Esther had recognized the barn; she actually knew the place quite well. As a child, she had tumbled in its hay and played hide-and-seek underneath its rafters. It was part of the property owned by a Christian farmer, a friend of her deceased father's, a kind man who lived 18 kilometers away from her hometown of Chelm, a town that was currently occupied and flooded by legions of Nazi soldiers.

"This is the place you'd escape to?" Esther's friend asked incredulously. "You'd have to be crazy . . . walking into the enemy's embrace. You might as well die here!"

"My mother didn't come to me for nothing," Esther said stubbornly. "If she told me to go to the barn, there must be a good reason. . . ."

On the morning of October 14, 1943, 300 inmates of Sobibor, armed with weapons smuggled into the camp by sympathetic partisans, revolted. Chaos erupted as phone wires were snipped, electric cables cut, guards overwhelmed, the Armory seized, Nazi soldiers shot, and hundreds of prisoners jumped the barbed wire fence. As Esther leaped to freedom and ran for cover to the adjoining woods, blood gushed from her scalp. She had always feared a bullet in her back; but when it came, it grazed her head instead.

Faint with hunger, weak from her injuries, Esther nonetheless prevailed. In the forest, she joined up with a group of partisans with whom she traveled. She hid by day and walked at night, and when the hunger and thirst drove her to the brink of madness, she knocked at the doors of the little farmhouses she passed, and mercifully, everyone was kind.

The partisans begged her to stay with them and become a permanent member of their group. She would be safer, much safer, they tried to convince her, if she hid in the woods and joined their cause. But Esther could not be deterred.

"I have to find the barn in the dream," she said stubbornly.

And two weeks later she did.

Beyond the edge of the woods where she walked, she finally saw the outlines of the structure she had so tenaciously sought. She waited until dusk, and then warily slipped inside. The barn was empty. She ascended the ladder to the loft, made a bed out of the hay, and then fell asleep.

The next day, she went hunting for food. A compassionate farmer gave her a loaf of bread and a bottle of milk, but when she returned to the loft to slowly savor her meal, an odd thing occurred. She placed the bottle of milk on top of a bale of hay while she tore into the bread, but when she turned to retrieve it, the bottle was gone. Somehow the mounds of hay enveloping her had swallowed the bottle up whole or else it had dropped to the floor below. Esther was frantic with thirst. She dug through the hay and hunted on the floor. All sense of caution was flung aside as she clawed at the floorboards in vain, making agitated noises as she dove deeper into the hay. Her movements grew louder and more careless with each passing moment, jolting awake the slumbering figure huddled in a corner on the other side of the barn.

"Who's there?!" the figure sprang up in alarm.

Now I'm finished, Esther thought.

"Who's there?" the menacing figure shouted once more.

Esther froze in shock.

"Yidel?" she cried in disbelief as she recognized her brother's unmistakable voice. "Yidel . . . is that you?"

"Esther!" he screamed. "Esther'le!"

"But Yidel . . . ," she labored slowly, incomprehensibly. "You're supposed to be dead!"

"No, Esther, you're the one who's dead!"

"They told me you were shot at the work camp . . . ," she said.

"Esther," he broke in gently, "I was the only one who escaped that night. Everyone else was killed. But Esther'le," he said, eyes brimming with tears, "someone told me that *you* were dead! I am overcome with joy that you are alive! But how did you know to come here?" Yidel asked in wonderment.

"Mama told me to," Esther explained. "She came to me in a dream. I'll tell you all about it soon. But first I want to know: how long have you been here?"

"Ten months. Papa's friend has been hiding me here since I escaped."

"Yidel!" Esther sobbed. "All I want you to do is sit with me all night and just hold my hand. . . . And then we'll watch the sun rise . . . together."

The next morning, the two heard a loud, sharp whistle coming from outside the barn. "That's a signal for me to come out," Yidel explained hurriedly to Esther. "It's Papa's friend, the farmer. He wants to talk to me."

The eyes of the farmer were tense and worried.

"I don't know if I can keep you here anymore," he said not unkindly. "A strange woman has been seen wandering nearby, and no one knows if she belongs to a partisan group or who she is. I'm worried that the neighbors will get suspicious."

"That woman is my sister!" Yidel cried. And he told the farmer the miraculous story of his sister, the dream, and her escape from Sobibor.

The farmer was visibly moved by Yidel's account.

"Well, if God brought you together," he said, "who am I to tear you apart? Your sister can stay with you in the barn."

And in that barn, thanks to the loving guidance of a mother who watched over her children from a world beyond, Esther and Yidel hid safely for nine more months, until they were liberated by the Russians and the war finally ground to its end.

More than half-a-century later, there are only 30 survivors of Sobibor left to tell the story, and Esther and Yidel are among them. For the siblings, every day is a continuing celebration of the miracle of mother love, a legacy that defies both time and memory.

❧

Comment

Even the dark veil of evil and the impenetrable wall of death can be pierced by the love of a mother for her children.

Everybody who knew Hazel Davis knew about her rings. There were four—all beautiful diamonds given to her by her late husband for anniversaries and birthdays.

Since her beloved's death, Hazel wore the rings every day, taking them off only to clean them, or, as she did one Sunday while on a drive, to put lotion on her hands. While her friend Irma drove, Hazel slipped off her rings and put them into her pocket.

"I'm starved," Irma said, pulling into a Cracker Barrel parking lot. The women were going to Virginia to visit Hazel's mom and had already traveled 100 miles from their North Carolina homes.

As Hazel scanned the menu, she reached into her pocket—and felt only a hole!

"Irma!" she choked.

The women scoured the parking lot and the van—in vain. As they drove along Route 40, Irma tried to console her friend.

But tears ran down Hazel's face. "I bet someone saw them and realized they were valuable," Hazel cried.

Little did she know how right she was. Minutes after Hazel and Irma left, the Reverend Jim Diehl and his wife Karen pulled into the Cracker Barrel on their way home from a trip with their boys. When they saw something glinting in the sun, they stopped—and found themselves staring at diamonds!

These mean a lot to someone, Karen knew, looking at the ring from Jim she wore on her left hand. "We have to find the owner," she said.

Over the next week, they spoke with the restaurant and the police, hoping someone had reported them missing. But Hazel hadn't. She was too upset and shaken that day to think straight and had left without notifying the restaurant of her loss. And once home, she figured whoever had found the rings had probably kept them.

The Diehls had indeed kept the rings—in a safe deposit box.

Five weeks later, Jim was at a hospital visiting a congregation member and his wife Linda. While chatting, Linda mentioned that her mother's friend had lost some valuable rings in a parking lot. Jim was shaken. It can't be, he told himself. He had found the rings 100 miles away. Yet he had to ask where the woman had lost them.

"At a Cracker Barrel in Statesville," Linda replied.

It seemed unbelievable, even to a man in the miracle business. But he asked for the woman's number.

When her phone rang and Jim's wife Karen gave her the news, Hazel wept with joy. And when she learned that her good Samaritans lived only miles away, she had to laugh.

"It's a miracle," she told the Diehls when they delivered her rings. "It just goes to prove that there are amazing, lovely people out there."

*O*ur friendship began with Joni's penpal ad in a monthly magazine. When I answered that ad several years ago, I never could have imagined the journey I was setting out upon! My first letter to her, one of introduction, went unanswered for three months. I'd long since forgotten writing it when her response finally arrived.

In spite of that slow start, we soon discovered much in common—a shared love of writing and music and gardening and needlework—but in many ways our lives were vastly different. She was 33 and recovering from a second abusive marriage and divorce; I was 10 years older and had been married since I was a teenager to the love of my life. Joni had routinely endured abuse I could scarcely imagine. She did not believe in God; I had a lifelong faith which, while shaky at times, had a firm foundation.

Our friendship flourished by way of the inky trail. We exchanged recipes and cross-stitch patterns and garden seeds. Our lives became happily entwined as our frequent letters traveled across the many miles between us. The friendship filled a need in both of us for that special relationship neither of us was fortunate enough to have with our biological sisters. She poured out her heart to me, as though the simple act of telling me the horrors of her life would somehow cleanse her soul and put her shattered hopes and dreams back together again. I listened and prayed and tried my best to help her find the peace she was so desperately searching for in her life. The long letters soon were interspersed with equally lengthy phone calls. We laughed and cried together, and though a thousand miles separated us, we became sisters of the heart.

In the summer of '96, Joni's world once again came crashing down around her as a relationship she was involved in abruptly ended. She became suicidal and many times in the wee hours of the mornings to follow, I found myself on the phone with her, reassuring my precious friend that she was loved and that her life could again be worth living. My insistence that she seek professional help fell on deaf ears. It seemed as though there was little I could do as I beseeched God to show me a way to help her.

One day I was walking through the mall with Joni very much on my mind. I wandered into a card shop, where my attention was immediately drawn to a music box on a shelf among many other music boxes. It was a small box with a short poem of friendship in its lid. As I opened it, my mind was filled with good memories as it played "You Are My Sunshine," a song I'd often sung to my children in their childhood years. I listened to the melody and then closed the lid and continued on my way. As I once again resumed my shopping, I felt the gentle touch of an unseen hand on my shoulder guiding me back to the shop and an urgent need to send that music box to Joni. I bought it and mailed it to her the following day.

Three days passed before I answered my phone to find Joni there crying. She managed, between her tears, to explain to me that she had decided to end her life and had made a list of 10 things she needed to do first. One item on that list was to hear the song "You Are My Sunshine" one last time. It was a song she'd loved as a child and it brought back happy memories of those days. Having it come to her as it did reminded her of the love of her faraway friend and prompted her to add one more thing to her list—she wanted to come meet me.

Two very long days later, Joni arrived on my doorstep. What a joy it was to finally meet this friend I'd come to love so dearly. We talked and cried and laughed a lot in the next five days and through the miracle of our friendship, she discovered a desire to live again. As for me, my faith in God was strengthened as I watched in amazement the way He used a simple childhood song in a music box sent to a friend. I learned never to doubt the stirrings of a small still voice or the touch of an angel's hand.

God truly does work in mysterious ways, or perhaps His answers to His children's heartfelt prayers are not so mysterious at all. Whatever the explanation, I thank Him for my friendship with Joni and for that tiny treasure of a music box.

—*Karen Briggs*

*S*he had felt an immediate kinship with him and thought the feeling was mutual.

He had taken an instant dislike to her and couldn't wait to take her back home.

The hours flew by for *her;* time had never seemed to pass so quickly.

To *him,* every minute was an eternity.

She wished the night would never end.

He was sorry it had ever begun.

Still, he was a gentleman and he didn't want to hurt her feelings. She was, after all, sweet and soft and kind— just not his type. He was attracted to women who were mysterious and aloof, confident and smug. The kind of women who never went out on blind dates set up by anxious friends.

When he had called her on Monday, he had detailed his plans for the Saturday night date, seeking her approval. Dinner, a Broadway show, dancing at the new club everyone was raving about. He couldn't back out of any of it now; it would be too much of a rebuff.

Her eyes lit up with joy as the evening stretched out before them; *his* glazed over with boredom.

Then the date was finally over. *She* sighed Too bad; *he* breathed Thank God! He drove her back to her home in Brooklyn and eagerly pushed the door handle on the driver's side so he could escort her inside.

There was one minor problem.

The car door was jammed.

"That's weird," he muttered, consternation flooding his face as he tried to jimmy the handle open.

It wouldn't budge.

He banged the door with his fist, kicked it with his foot, shoved it with his shoulder. To no avail. It was absolutely, positively, and very mysteriously, stuck.

Flustered, he turned to her with his apologies.

"Sorry," he said, "but we'll have to go out through the door on your side. Do you mind?"

She tugged at the handle, and he waited for the door to swing wide open, offering deliverance and escape.

Her door wouldn't budge, either.

"This is so bizarre!" he exclaimed. "We went in and out of the car at least a half dozen times tonight, and there was nothing wrong with either door. There wasn't even a hint of any problem. I just don't understand it. It's not as if it's icy outside or freezing. Why should the doors jam right now?"

The car was a two-door model. It was the middle of the night, and they were in the middle of a very quiet, middle-class Brooklyn neighborhood. The houses lining the block were dark; none blazed with light or life. Not a single soul seemed to be stirring on the sleepy, deserted street. It was in the days before cell phones, and as frantic for flight as he was, he knew it would be cruel and unfair to use his horn to signal trouble and wake up the sleeping residents. Deliverance from his date might have to be postponed awhile.

"Well," he said, turning to her with a rueful smile, "I guess we'll just have to wait until someone drives by and rescues us. . . . I'm sure there are other young people on the block who stay out late on Saturday night."

"I don't know . . . ," she said hesitantly. "Most of the people living on this street are pretty elderly."

Inwardly, he shuddered. Outwardly, he flashed her a dazzlingly false grin that in her naiveté she took to be genuine.

"But hey," she said, brightening at the prospect of spending more time with him, "we can get a chance to truly talk now. . . . The show and the dancing were great, but they didn't give us much time to really get to know each other. . . . So tell me," she said, turning to him with an open, interested smile, "what do you think of . . .?"

Better make the best of it, he groaned, resigning himself to a few hours of boredom. But as she drew him into the conversation, he found himself increasingly enchanted by her candor, her little enthusiasms, her vivacity. She was intelligent, well-read, easygoing. And she was, to be fair, a really good sport about the jammed doors. Maybe he had misjudged her. Maybe it had been unfair to dismiss her so quickly. Maybe first impressions weren't the right impressions, after all. Maybe he would even ask her out . . . again.

It's been 10 years since that fateful night, and they've been happily married for the last nine and a half.

They never could figure out why the car doors jammed that night, but actually, in retrospect, they're glad they did.

❧

Comment
No way out may very well be the only way in.

As young Navy wives in Norfolk, Virginia, my neighbor Darleen and I developed a close bond. We even shared the same due date for our second babies. We each already had a daughter, so we were both thinking "blue."

Then, four months into my pregnancy, I miscarried. Darleen consoled me, but I still felt a pang of jealousy when she gave birth to a beautiful boy. As my two-year-old daughter, Cyndi, sat in a rocking chair cuddling baby Jimmy, I broke down. *God*, I prayed, *please let me be happy for Darleen.*

Darleen put her arms around me.

"I'll always share my son with you," she promised.

Just as Jimmy was taking his first wobbly steps, Darleen moved to Kansas. We kept in touch, but it took us 15 years to arrange a trip to visit. I couldn't believe my eyes when I saw handsome, almost-grown Jimmy.

Shortly after, we moved to North Carolina, where we got word that Jimmy had joined the Navy and was stationed nearby. On his first leave, he didn't have enough time to make it back home to Kansas, so he came to stay with us.

"He always has a home here," I wrote to Darleen.

Jimmy started coming to visit quite a bit. He palled around with Cyndi, and they became fast friends. But then I noticed something more: Cyndi and Jimmy were in love.

On their wedding day, I remembered Darleen's promise to me all those years before: "I'll always share my son with you."

Today we also share two grandsons.

—*Evelyn Myer Allison*

ge gege

Comment

Promises from the heart reach far beyond their own intent.

*W*hen the blizzard of '56 hit New Haven, dumping an unprecedented 25 inches of snow, schoolchildren squealed with delight. School was canceled for days on end, and the city ground to a virtual halt. The children pulled out their rusty sleds from basement storage spaces and frolicked in the snow, while in the municipal garages the city's snowplows stood helpless. Adults, liberated from grueling routine, welcomed the respite, excited at the winter wonderland that had descended on them. But inside one house, a woman peered anxiously outside as the snow continued to fall.

Beverly Liebowitz* had given birth to her first and only son one week before. As is customary in Jewish homes, the infant was to be named—and circumcised—in a religious ceremony called a *bris*. It was a momentous event in the life of a Jew—a major milestone of ritual consecration, a significant rite of passage in which family and community were expected to participate joyously.

But all night long, the snow had continued to fall unabated, and by morning the streets had not been cleared. The city had been rendered immobile, its public transportation system completely crippled.

For two days and nights, Mrs. Liebowitz had cleaned and scoured, peeled and grated, cooked and baked—and a dazzling display of delicacies and confections covered her dining room and kitchen tables. But now she wondered: Would anyone be able to come to the *bris*?

Her closest friends lived far away. Men tended to be more stalwart about trudging through drifts, mounds, hills of snow . . . she was sure that at least the required *minyan* (quorum of 10 men) would faithfully appear. But how many women would brave the dizzying white of the day? How many women could she count on to attend this most momentous event, one in which she longed for some female company of her own?

Miraculously, there were *three*. Three intrepid souls who knew how much their presence—or absence— would mean to Beverly Liebowitz. Three steadfast, loyal, tenacious women who slipped, skidded, and stumbled their way to Mrs. Liebowitz's door, wet snow clinging to their hair, faces, and clothing, laughing as they tramped inside and shook themselves free of the snow.

"Why, Judy Herman!"* Beverly shouted, jubilant, when she spotted her first friend. "I can't believe it . . . you live a mile away!"

"I wouldn't miss your son's *bris* for anything!" Judy smiled, bending over to give Beverly a wet kiss.

"Sara Glick!"* Beverly exclaimed a few minutes later when she saw her close friend framed in the doorway. "I thought you were still recovering from the minor surgery you had last week!"

"Wild horses couldn't keep me away!" Sara laughed, enfolding her friend in a warm embrace.

"Miriam Segal,* is that really you . . . or is it a mirage?" Beverly whooped again in excitement a few minutes later. "How on earth did you get here? You live almost two miles away!"

"Hey, Beverly," Miriam laughed, "I'd walk halfway across the world for you, don't you know that?"

These were the three women who showed, and Beverly felt loved and grateful. She knew what a tremendous sacrifice they had made for her, and she felt blessed to have such loving friends.

But as it turned out, Beverly wasn't the only one to be blessed that day. It seems that her little house, so radiant with joy, so aglow with love, and so luminous with the warmth of special friends, had become a vessel that day—a cornucopia of blessings that filled up, overflowed, and inundated all those within its reach.

Nine months after her own son's *bris*, Beverly Liebowitz was kept busy one morning rushing to three different *brises* taking place all over town.

Her first stop was a local synagogue where the Herman family's *bris* was being held. Judy Herman had had six little girls in rapid succession; this was her first son.

Next Beverly headed for a small catering hall where the Glick *bris* was taking place. Sara Glick had had two children—now teenagers—and then none had followed; she had been suffering from secondary infertility and had been unable to conceive another child for the last eight years.

Miriam Segal had been *childless* for 10. The Segal *bris* that Beverly attended later that morning was perhaps the most joyous affair of all.

Nine months after they had attended the Liebowitz *bris* and drunk from the goblet that contained the ritual wine used in the ceremony, all three women—Judy Herman, Sara Glick, and Miriam Segal—bore sons and had *bris* ceremonies of their own.

Beverly Liebowitz had always felt indebted to the three and wished she could repay their extraordinary kindness. Miraculously, it seemed, she had accomplished her goal.

Comment

Little gestures of love sometimes require large doses of effort, but they yield unimaginable rewards.

*S*eventeen Christmases ago, Carol Hughes snapped a photo of her one-year-old niece Lisa as the chubby-cheeked, green-eyed toddler danced on a table in Hugheses' farmhouse.

When the shutter snapped, Carol Hughes had no idea that the photos of Lisa, playing dress-up with a blonde wig, a big straw bonnet, and a pair of Carol's white high heels, would be all she would have to remember her niece.

She also had no way of knowing that copies of the same photos, now sepia-hued with age, would ultimately reunite her with the child she had raised as her own daughter before Carol's sister, Kathleen Abraham, now deceased, surrendered Lisa for adoption in 1977.

Carol Hughes and her former husband Bill had nurtured Lisa as their own daughter for the year that Kathleen was hospitalized with severe mental illness.

Two days after Kathleen was released from the hospital, she called county authorities and surrendered Lisa for adoption without telling her sister or anyone in the family.

"Kathleen wanted Lisa to be away from her because she loved her and didn't want her to deal with her illness," Carol said. "If Lisa stayed with me, she thought, she would make my life and Lisa's a living hell."

Bureaucracy ultimately prevented the Hugheses from adopting the baby. Because they lived in a different county from Kathleen, they were not on the adoptive parents waiting list. A judge denied Carol custody of her niece.

A heartbroken Carol said she did all she could do. "I wanted Lisa to know that she was loved and that she was wanted." Carol prepared a package with one of three silver lockets with Lisa's picture (the other two stayed with Carol and Kathleen), her christening gown, which Carol had sewn, Lisa's "beany doll," and an album of photos of Lisa taken throughout the year she spent with the Hugheses. She sent the "love package" with a plea to Lisa's caseworker that it would go to whomever adopted Lisa.

"Lisa was born on October 13, 1976, which is my younger son Archie's birthday," Carol said. "My sister brought Lisa home from the hospital and put the baby in his arms and told Archie that Lisa was his baby. Until his 12th birthday, Archie asked Santa Claus to bring him back his little sister."

Carol tearfully recalled the years the family bought birthday cakes each October to celebrate Lisa's birthday.

Time never seemed to heal Carol's fears for Lisa. "Every time I saw items on the news about adoptive and foster children being abused my heart ached, and I prayed that God had given Lisa a good family who loved her and that somehow Lisa knew she was not given away because she was unwanted," Carol said.

On the afternoon of January 5, 1995, Carol received "a true miracle in answer to all my prayers."

Carol was sitting outside during a break from her job as a librarian at the Clayton County Headquarters Library, sharing a story with a young coworker, Lisa Lapham, who'd started working there just 10 days earlier.

Carol, who had just gone through a rough period that included a divorce and major surgery, was telling Lisa the happy-ending story of a library patron's reunion with her birth family.

Lisa told Carol that the story gave her chills because she had also been adopted.

But what Lisa said next nearly made Carol fall over. "She said she must have been a ham when she was a baby because she had photos of herself in a long blonde wig."

Carol sat stunned for a moment and then began describing the photos.

"I said yes to every detailed description," Lisa said, "and asked: 'Are you my mother?' I knew without seeing the pictures that I had found my family."

Lisa is brunette and tall like Carol and her arched brows and green eyes are like those of the toddler in the matched sets of photos the two compared that afternoon.

Both women say one of the most emotional highlights of the reunion was when Carol set the silver locket photo of Lisa in her niece's palm.

"I could see arms and legs of other people in my baby pictures," Lisa said, "and I would sit for hours and wonder whose legs and arms they were—my mother's? My brother's? It's so wonderful to see who they belonged to."

"After all the years of thinking about this child on birthdays and at Christmas and all the years of praying that God had given her good parents and a good life, God brought this child right here—to my library," Carol said. "And after meeting the wonderful people that have done such a wonderful job of raising this beautiful 19-year-old young lady, I know my prayers were always heard."

Charlie and Darlene Lipham adopted Lisa after six years of trying to have children and four years of waiting on the adoptive parents list in their county. Darlene said the call announcing Lisa's arrival in their life came after the couple had nearly given up hope. "We'd torn our house apart in a remodeling project after we'd started thinking it would be another four years before we actually had a child," she said. "I got the call and I yelled, 'We have a little girl,' and thought 'Great, my house is upside down.' "

Two weeks *before* Lisa fatefully found Carol Hughes, she had called the state to find out about tracing her birth parents. She'd been told that there was a two-year waiting list and that she'd have to have her parents' permission to begin the search because Lisa had not turned 21. Darlene Lipham said she supported her daughter's decision to begin looking, but never expected to face Lisa's birth family so soon.

—*Christi Conner*

$\mathcal{I}$n 1987, Sister Barbara Cox, a member of the Dominican Sisters of Springfield, Illinois, was cleaning the convent's pantry when she came across a placard lying upside down under the shelf paper.

Hmm, that's strange, she thought, as she tugged at the poster wedged deep inside the shelf. *What could this be?*

It turned out to be a poster demonstrating the Heimlich maneuver—the kind of poster that one ordinarily finds hanging in restaurants and coffee shops, places where vulnerable patrons are in danger of choking on food.

Wonder how it got here? she mused. *It looks old and musty. . . . Wonder how long it's been here? . . . Well, it's not doing anyone any good lying under the shelf paper,* Sister Barbara decided. *Might as well hang it up myself. But where?*

The outside of the pantry door didn't seem appropriate. It was too public a place. *After all, we're a convent, not a restaurant,* she reasoned. *I'll just hang it up inside the door, in case we ever need it.*

She affixed it to the inside of the door and then closed the door. She meant to tell the other sisters about her discovery of the poster and about what she had done with it, but she had many other things on her mind that day, and she simply forgot. Consequently, nobody else in the convent knew about the poster's existence.

The next day, Sister Barbara was eating lunch with the other nuns in the convent and talking rather quickly and animatedly. Suddenly, she started choking on a piece of food, and, embarrassed, she fled to the kitchen to clear her throat. But as much as she tried, she couldn't drive the morsel of food out of her windpipe where it had stubbornly lodged.

She thought she would clear her throat and expel the food on her own, but with a sinking feeling she realized that her situation was far more serious than she had first imagined. She couldn't seem to breathe, and when she tried to call out to the sisters in the dining room, she wasn't able to vocalize. She couldn't talk at all.

No air was going in or out of her windpipe and she was feeling lightheaded and faint. Panic-stricken, Sister Barbara signaled to the other sisters that she needed help. They rushed into the kitchen, but looked at her helplessly. None of them were trained in first aid techniques, and none had ever treated a choking emergency. They didn't know what to do or how to assist her. It was then that she remembered the poster that she had pasted inside the pantry door.

She pointed frantically at the closed pantry door. No one understood why. She continued to gesticulate toward the door until, finally, one of the sisters opened it. There they saw the poster demonstrating the Heimlich maneuver and understood that it could save her life.

Sister Clara, one of the tiniest sisters in the convent—all of five feet to Sister Barbara's five feet six—read the instructions aloud while following them in a concentrated and deliberate manner, one at a time, step by step. She did exactly as the poster advised, and though it was her first time performing the Heimlich maneuver, she was successful. A piece of food came flying out of Sister Barbara's mouth, and the emergency was over.

"There's no question in my mind that this was providential," reflects Sister Barbara. "The timing was impeccable. I just happened upon the poster the previous day, and the very next day I was its beneficiary. . . . I do believe that I was meant to live a little bit longer. If I hadn't found the Heimlich poster the day before and impulsively pasted it on the inside of the pantry door, I doubt if I would be alive today."

While finishing up a one-day business trip to Los Angeles, my husband, Bob, and I discovered that our meeting site was about 10 minutes from my grandmother's nursing home. We had only an hour before boarding our flight home to Walla Walla, hardly enough time to visit her. But something deep within me said, *Take the time.*

We hadn't seen Grandma in years, not since her mind began to fail. She didn't recognize her own son or remember that her husband was dead. Surely she wouldn't know us. We planned to be back in L.A. in a few months and could spend more time with her then. *Why go now?* I asked myself as we made our way through L.A. traffic. I looked at my watch.

At the nursing home, we found Grandma asleep in her wheelchair. I walked over and gently touched her on the shoulder. "Grandma? Grandma?"

She awoke, blinked a few times and looked hard at me. Then her eyes filled with wonder. "Barbara? Is that really you?" Grandma not only recognized Bob and me, she was absolutely lucid! She wanted to know everything about us. We reminisced about the times I had stayed with her when I was a child. The trips we made to Yosemite every summer. We talked about my grandfather. About what she thought heaven must be like. And how much she wanted to go there, to be with him again.

I had forgotten all about the time until Bob reminded me we had a plane to catch. Grandma hugged us and saw us off.

The day after we got home, my father called to say that Grandma had had a massive stroke. The next morning she slipped into heaven.

It would have been so easy not to stop and see Grandma that day. But we'd obeyed the nudge of the Spirit. And an hour had become a lifelong memory.

—*Barbara Deal*

Comment

Nudges of the spirit are signs in Braille for the visually impaired soul. Without them, we stumble eternally in a maze of darkness.

*M*y granddaughter Tate turned five years old recently, and her mother gave her a very special present: a pair of red cowgirl boots that had been her own when she was a little girl. Tate pulled on the little red boots and began to dance around the room. It is always fun to dress up in Mom's clothes when you are a little girl, but when Mom's clothes are your own size, well, the excitement is almost uncontainable.

Kelly, my daughter-in-law, told us about the first time she wore her boots. You see, not only did she experience the thrill of wearing her first pair of real cowgirl boots; she also experienced the thrill of meeting her first love.

She was five and he was seven. He lived in the city and his father brought him to Kelly's grandfather's farm one Saturday afternoon to ride the horses. Kelly sat on the top fence rail as Grandfather saddled her pony. She was trying very hard not to get her shiny new boots dirty when the city boy came over to say hello. He smiled at her and admired her new boots. It must have been love at first sight, because Kelly offered to let him ride her pony. She had never let anyone ride her pony before.

Later that year, Grandfather sold the farm, and Kelly didn't see the young boy again. But Kelly never forgot that magical moment in her childhood, and she thought of the city boy every time she put on her red cowgirl boots. When she outgrew them, her mother packed them away. Years later, while organizing for a garage sale, Kelly found the little red boots and decided to give them to Tate for her birthday.

Tate's laughter brought us back to the present. My son, Marty, scooped his giggling daughter into his arms and danced around the room with her. "I do like your new cowgirl boots, baby," he said. "They remind me of the day I rode my very first pony. I wasn't much older than you."

"Is this a true story, Daddy? Or a make-believe one?" Tate loved to listen to her daddy tell stories about when he was a little boy. "Does it have a happy ending?" Then she begged him to tell her about his first pony ride. Marty smiled at Tate's unending string of questions as he sat down in the big, comfortable recliner. Tate climbed up into his lap.

"Once upon a time when I was seven years old, I lived in the big city called St. Louis. That's in Missouri. I wanted a horse more than anything in the world, but we couldn't have one in the city. I told my dad that I wanted to be a real cowboy when I grew up, so that summer he took me to a farm not very far from here. And I got to ride a real pony for the very first time."

You can guess how Marty's story ends, but as incredible as it sounds, Marty and Kelly had no idea they had met as children until the day of their daughter's fifth birthday.

True stories have happy endings, too!

— *Jeannie Williams*

Comment

The ending of a cosmic tale is often delayed but always worth the wait.

"*That* one, Mom!" 13-year-old Jacob Powers cried as he leaned over the pen of squirming puppies. Jacob was pointing to the mangy runt of the litter, sitting apart from her siblings, sad and sickly.

That's the sorriest little dog I've ever seen, Mary Ann Powers thought. "I don't know . . . ," she began.

"But if we don't take her, she's going to die!" Jacob cried, prompting his mom to look again. The pup gazed back with woeful brown eyes. Suffering from mange and malnutrition, she'd probably be put to sleep. But a little TLC might do wonders, Mary Ann decided.

They named the puppy Shelly, and Mary Ann nursed her back to health. In time, she grew into a frisky pet who loved to go fishing with Mary Ann's fiancé Bart. She followed Mary Ann everywhere, then settled each night in the doggie bed Mary Ann set up in the room next to hers.

Then one night, Mary Ann awoke at 1:30 A.M. with a burning in her chest and a shooting pain in her arm. *It's just heartburn,* she thought. But the pain grew worse. *Something's wrong!* she realized, stumbling toward the family room. *Could I be having a heart attack? I'm only 44!*

"Bart!" she tried to gasp, but couldn't. *I'm going to die!* she panicked as the room spun. Suddenly, she heard a whine—and felt a wet nose. Shelly! And then darkness closed in.

Shelly whined as she gazed at Mary Ann. *Wake up!* her worried eyes seemed to say. Shelly raced for the bedroom.

Bart was sleeping when he felt something wet licking his hand. He opened his eyes and saw Shelly, who began to whine. *What?* he thought, confused. Shelly wasn't usually in the bedroom at night.

Shelly whined, stared at Bart, and looked meaningfully at the door. Bart rose and followed her to the family room. His heart nearly stopped when he saw Mary Ann crumpled in a heap.

She's still breathing, thank God! he thought with relief as he knelt beside her. He rushed her to the Emergency Room, where doctors discovered she'd suffered a near-fatal heart attack. They performed emergency surgery to insert a shunt that would keep Mary Ann's heart ventricle open. "It was a success," they told Bart. "But it's a good thing you got her here so quickly—there wasn't a moment to waste."

Bart knew who they had to thank. "If it weren't for Shelly, you wouldn't be here," he told Mary Ann.

Back home two days later, Mary Ann hugged Shelly. "You saved my life!" she whispered as Shelly wriggled with joy.

Mary Ann, Bart, and Jacob showered special treats on Shelly—and Mary Ann still brings home special rewards each time she goes to the grocery store.

"It's my way of saying thanks," she explains. "I owe Shelly my life!"

—*Peg Verone*

*H*ospital waiting rooms may vary in size and décor, but in atmosphere they're all basically the same. The mood is tense, serious, fearful. People pace nervously, glance at their watches; they stare into space; they weep quietly. The waiting room is the place where destinies change forever. And it's the place where Carmen Maloney met Bob Bradshaw for the first time in January 1998.

The University of Maryland Medical Center has waiting rooms on every floor, but both had separately chosen to retreat to the first-floor visitors' atrium. Carmen was huddled in a corner, crying softly; Bob, watching from afar, was struck by her despair. Most people steer clear of their weeping neighbors, but Bob Bradshaw reached out. "What's the matter?" he gently asked, leaning toward Carmen compassionately.

"It's my mother," she sobbed. "She's been here since October waiting for a heart transplant. If she doesn't get one soon, she'll die."

Carmen's mother, Bobbie diSabbatino, was 56 years old and had had a massive heart attack in October 1997. She had been confined to the cardiac care unit of the hospital ever since, waiting for a heart that would match her blood type and size. She had been added to a waiting list that stretched four thousand names long, and the odds were that she would die before the perfect match was found for her.

Throughout her life, Bobbie had been extraordinarily devoted to her daughter, Carmen, who was now 31. When Carmen's first marriage had failed, Bobbie had taken her daughter and grandchild into her home until the two had been able to get back on their feet. Carmen couldn't bear the thought of her mother slipping away from her like this. Her mother *had* to live; she *needed* her mother to live!

After pouring her heart out to Bob Bradshaw and being comforted by his empathy, Carmen noticed his own dazed and stricken look. The emotional combat fatigue straining his features indicated that he was not an expectant father eagerly awaiting news of the birth of his child. Something far more serious had brought him to this waiting room today, Carmen realized—so, gently, she too made inquiries.

"My wife has a rare brain defect," he answered, "but the doctors say they can treat it. She should be out of here in a week."

Cheryl Bradshaw had always been healthy and robust, but a few weeks earlier she had suddenly begun experiencing debilitating headaches. Then she had had a grand mal seizure that brought her to the hospital. A CAT scan revealed the startling news that the 38-year-old woman had been born with an *arteriovenous malformation*— a rare brain defect that deprives the brain of blood—and that she had been living on borrowed time.

"My God," a radiologist gasped when he read the CAT scan. "How has this woman been able to survive all these years?"

The defect was so advanced that the only option now was a 27-hour, two-part operation, but doctors were confident that it would be successful and that Cheryl would make a complete recovery.

Carmen was happy, for Bob's sake, that the prospects for his wife's recovery were good. By contrast, her own mother's chances for survival grew slimmer every day.

After a long conversation, Carmen and Bob finally rose from their seats in the visitors' lounge, bade each other good luck, and said good-bye. They never expected to see each other again.

But over the next few days, they kept running into each other. They always seemed to be headed for the same bank of elevators, the same hospital corridor, or the same waiting room at the exact same time. And soon they developed a special bond, as they tried by turns to support one another, offer hope, and provide cheer.

Bob spoke often of his four children: Kristen, 12; Sara, 10; Kyle, 7; and his 19-year-old stepdaughter, Sherrie Waldrup, Cheryl's daughter by a previous marriage. Carmen shared stories about her son. And they promised each other that when their loved ones finally recovered and were discharged from the hospital, they would all go out together and celebrate.

But one morning, Carmen entered the atrium and found the usually optimistic Bob dissolved in tears. In the aftermath of the operation, it seemed, Cheryl's brain had started hemorrhaging. She was now in a coma and on life support.

Each day after that, Bob provided Carmen with updates whenever they encountered one another. And by now they were running into each other so regularly that each no longer feigned surprise when they saw the other in the lounge.

"Cheryl's coming out of the coma!" Bob told Carmen excitedly one day. "I read her a get well card that our daughter Sara had sent, and tears rolled down her face as I read it. And then . . . Sara had asked at the end: 'Mommy, if you like this card, please squeeze Daddy's hand.' And she did! Cheryl squeezed my hand!" He added, "The doctors say that Cheryl's making rapid strides, and we should begin discussing plans for rehabilitation soon."

But on February 9, 1998, the worst-case scenario for Cheryl Bradshaw occurred. Her brain ruptured, in what doctors call a "lethal bleed." This time, there was nothing that they could do but helplessly watch her fade away.

On February 11, Bob Bradshaw finally faced the truth: This time, there would be no miraculous recoveries, no sudden reversals, no inexplicable changes-for-the-better. Cheryl Bradshaw was on an irrevocable journey toward death.

And it was then that Bob Bradshaw, who always thought of other people first—even in the throes of deepest grief—thought of seeking out the nurse in charge of organ donations.

Cheryl had always been a fervent exponent of organ donation. She believed that donating your organs was a way of doing service—a final gift to the world from beyond the grave. Bob knew that Cheryl would want him to proceed with the plan he had just outlined in his head.

Bob found the nurse in charge of organ donations and made his unusual request. He wanted to donate his wife's organs when she expired. The nurse nodded. But Cheryl's heart, he added—he wanted to donate her heart to someone specific. . . . Could that be done? The nurse stared at him, nonplussed.

Direct donations of organs to specific recipients was almost unheard-of, she explained. *In fact, she had never seen it done. But technically, she didn't see why it **couldn't** be done.*

She hastily referred him to Dr. Ronald Freudenberger, medical director of cardiac transplantation, and Dr. John Conte, director of heart and lung transplantation. Dr. Conte had performed 150 transplant operations, but none like the one Bob Bradshaw had in mind. And Dr. Freudenberger stated that the chances of the match's being perfect, in terms of organ and body size, were about one in a million.

But Bob Bradshaw was not discouraged, nor was he deterred by the daunting statistics. Carmen Maloney had opened his heart to the plight of her mother. And now he wanted to bequeath to her the ultimate gift of his heart — the one belonging to his cherished wife.

As doctors made arrangements for organ matching tests, Bob raced downstairs to the visitors' atrium where he was certain he would find Carmen. At first, she couldn't comprehend what Bob was telling her. She cried on hearing that Cheryl was near death. And she cried even more when Bob told her that he wanted to give Cheryl's heart to Carmen's mother. "No one has ever given me a gift like this before," she sobbed.

Miraculously, Cheryl Bradshaw's heart proved to be a perfect match for Bobbie diSabbatino. Carmen's mother underwent the successful operation on February 14 — Valentine's Day.

At Cheryl Bradshaw's funeral a few days later, the Bradshaw children sang their favorite song from the movie *Titanic* — Celine Dion's beloved "My Heart Will Go On."

Comment

A heart that feels another's pain is often blessed with the power to heal it.

*S*ue and Kenny Burton had tried for more than two years to have a baby, and things weren't going well. Month after month, despite many medical tests, they continued to be disappointed. People in their tiny, close-knit town of Frankfort, Kansas, knew about the Burtons' dream and were praying for them.

At that time, Sue was singing contemporary Christian songs in a sextet formed by women from Frankfort's United Methodist Church. The group, ironically named Special Delivery, performed regularly at mother-daughter banquets, Elk and Moose club meetings, and other functions. "Usually during a program we could each share a little personal history with the audience," Sue explains. "Since we ranged from teenager to grandmother status, people could relate to all of us."

The other singers, knowing Sue's longing for a baby, encouraged her to share that with audiences too, and she did. The response was tremendously supportive. After the Christmas concerts, many people came up to assure Sue that they would add their prayers to those of her neighbors. In March, a woman from South Dakota even predicted that at this time next year, Sue would have a baby daughter. Although Sue and Kenny seemed no closer to decorating a nursery, it helped to know so many people cared.

On Mother's Day weekend, Sue drove her mother to Kansas City to spend some time with Sue's sister, Shelley, who attended college there. The three visited shopping malls all day Saturday, and Sue conscientiously pressed the automatic door lock every time they parked and got out of her car. "We joked about being overly cautious in the Big City, but there was no point in being careless," Sue says.

Sunday morning, the trio awakened to a steady rain. They lounged around in Shelley's apartment and had an early lunch. The downpour continued, so eventually the three decided to go out anyway. Dodging raindrops, they splashed across the parking lot to Sue's car. "Hurry up! I'm getting soaked!" Shelley laughed as Sue unlocked the driver's door, then pressed the switch to open the other doors.

Shelley scrambled into the front seat, while their mother got in back. "Look at this!" she exclaimed as her daughters turned around. On the back seat was a pink baby bootie.

"Where did that come from?" Sue asked. "It wasn't there yesterday, was it, Mom?"

"No," her mother said. "I was in and out of here all day, and I never saw it."

"Could it have been stuck down in the seat, maybe left by one of your friends in Frankfort?" Shelley wondered.

Sue shook her head. "I doubt it. My friends' children are all older. I don't think a baby has ever been in this car."

The women pondered over that awhile.

"Someone must have found it lying near the car just now and tossed it in, thinking it was ours," Shelley tried again.

"But," Sue pointed out, "the car was never open—you know I've locked the doors whenever we got out. And why would anyone think a bootie belonged to us? No one here knows us."

"Look how muddy and wet it is outside," Sue's mother added. "But this bootie is clean and dry."

The women fell silent again, turning over possible explanations in their minds. But no solution emerged. The bootie's position looked deliberate, as if someone had wanted to be sure it was seen.

"What if . . .?" Sue couldn't finish her sentence. But the others knew what she was thinking. Was the bootie a message from heaven, a sign that all those prayers ascending from the Kansas plains were about to be answered?

Sue hardly dared to hope. She took the bootie home, put it in her Bible, and waited. Waited until she realized she was indeed pregnant, had been pregnant on that Mother's Day morning, and would, just as the lady from South Dakota predicted, be a mother—of a daughter—very soon. "When people asked how I could be so sure of a girl, I would simply show them the bootie," Sue says. "Would God send pink for any other reason?"

Today, five years later, the bootie hangs over Paige Elizabeth Burton's bed as a constant reminder that God answers prayers. In fact, he answers in abundance, for Paige now has a little sister. "I have no doubt that an angel left the bootie there as a sign for me," Sue says.

For Sue, every day is Mother's Day.

—Joan Wester Anderson

I stared hard at the old color photograph, a deep yearning welling up inside me. The young girl burst joyously from the water. As she opened her eyes, a look of utter surprise lit up her face. Because directly in front of her, suspended in mid-air, was a large, sleek bottlenose dolphin. That young girl was *me*. And after all these years I was still in love with dolphins.

Now, 23 years later, sitting alone in my small, one bedroom Manhattan apartment, I felt utterly miserable. Where had my dream gone? What happened to that fiery passion?

Perhaps it was all the disappointments. At 17, I wrote letters to every marine biologist in the country, begging for an opportunity to be with dolphins. "Your enthusiasm is refreshing," they wrote back, "but we can't help." At 19, I dropped out of college, moved to Florida to try to get hired by the Miami Seaquarium as one of those "sea maids" who smile a lot and toss the dolphins fish. Every day I rode my bike to the Seaquarium and every day they'd say, *sorry, no openings.* Eventually, I returned home defeated. With no handsome men banging down my door, I became self-sufficient as a writer.

But my love for dolphins never diminished. I began writing romance novels, and the one that did the best — published in 1981 and translated into seven languages — was titled *Lured into Dawn*, and written under the pen name Catherine Mills. It told the story of a New York business woman who falls madly in love with a dolphin trainer. While the heroine, Melinda Matthews, didn't exactly resemble me—she was tall, lithe, blonde, and the CEO of a successful New York cosmetic company, while I'm short, chunky, brunette, and deeply in debt—at least we shared common initials—MM. During a business trip to the lush island of Jamaica, she meets the ruggedly handsome Richard Carson, a seasoned dolphin trainer who worked at Sea Life Park, Jamaica—a fictional Montego Bay aquarium I made up out of my imagination. Of course in the end, they live happily ever after on a lush tropical island. The opening of the book describes their first unforgettable encounter. A frisky dolphin in a petting pool splashes Melinda, drenching her from head to toe. With her expensive silk dress clinging provocatively to her body, Melissa blushes beet red when she looks up and notices Richard staring at her. You can guess what happens after that . . .

Yet despite the book's international success, here I was, almost 10 years later, living alone in a noisy city crowded with eight million people and not one single dolphin (or ruggedly handsome boyfriend) in sight.

One warm summer night, I was absolutely miserable, feeling as if I had made an irrevocable mistake in my life. The only remnants of my passion were dolphin posters covering my stark white walls and a few ceramic dolphin knickknacks collecting dust on my shelves. Somehow I

had come to the painful realization that I never wanted
to be a writer. That I didn't want to live alone in a big
city. What I deeply wanted was to live by the sea, with a
man I totally loved and admired, surrounded by those
warm blooded mammals who felt like my true family.

As the clock approached midnight, I lay awake
feeling sorry for myself. I was too old to move to Miami
and become a sea maid. Who would hire a chunky lady
in her late 30s! I didn't want to become a biologist. All I
wanted was to be with dolphins, the way you want to be
near people you love.

Out of desperation, I called out to God. In the past,
in times of deep need, God had come through for me,
though always in ways I least expected.

"Please God," I whispered, "help me be with dolphins."

I slept late the next day. By the time I got up, it was
near 11 A.M. Outside the skies were heavy with the
threat of rain. As I sat dunking my tea bag into my
dolphin ceramic mug, I suddenly heard a voice. *"Go to the
New York Aquarium,"* it said. Puzzled, I looked around.
The voice wasn't exactly outside of me, but it wasn't
inside, either. What a silly idea, I thought. The New
York Aquarium was in Coney Island, Brooklyn. The
neighborhood turned dangerous after dark and it took
hours to get there by subway. Besides, I thought, all it
had were a bunch of fish behind glass walls. I went back
to sipping my tea. But again the voice intruded. *"Go to the
New York Aquarium."*

Yet still I argued against it. *I don't know how to get there. It's too far and too late to go.* When the voice loudly insisted a third time, I jumped to my feet. "All right!" I shot back. I called the Aquarium, got directions, and reluctantly left the house.

A few hours later, I hurried to the entrance, paid my fee and wandered inside. After walking through a dark corridor filled with fish tanks I found myself standing in front of a large outdoor aqua-theater. And there, just beyond the low metal gate, splashing around in a large concrete pool, were three bottlenose dolphins. My heart nearly burst with joy. God had led me to the only dolphins in New York!

The next show wasn't for 40 minutes so I climbed to the top of the bleachers and watched, mesmerized, as the dolphins entertained me. Minutes later, a young man in a red tee shirt emblazoned with the words "New York Aquarium" entered the aqua-theater. He was busying himself with some task when suddenly the voice returned, pushier than ever. *"Go talk to him."* Instinctively I resisted. No way, I thought. *"Go talk to him!"* the voice insisted again. I felt stupid and shy. What would I say to him? But when the voice intruded a third time, I stood up and headed over to him. "Excuse me," I said to the young man, not having any idea what I was going to say. "Do you . . . uh . . . work with these dolphins?" Before long we were having a conversation about a volunteer program where people could assist the dolphin trainers.

He might as well have told me I won the million dollar lottery. I could barely contain my excitement. "Don't get your hopes up, " he urged, "volunteering is not about playing with dolphins. They hardly ever let you near them. They're extremely picky about who gets chosen."

Well, he could have said I needed to scale Mount Everest. Somehow I would have found a way. Needless to say, I got hired to work every Wednesday. It didn't matter that I'd have to leave Manhattan before dawn. It didn't matter that I'd have to stand on my feet eight hours a day in a stainless steel feed room, defrosting hundreds of pounds of frozen mackerel, cleaning out plastic buckets thick with fish blood, or hauling large garbage bags of trash. What mattered was I knew my dolphins were always nearby.

Those Wednesdays changed my life. When friends saw me at a party a few weeks later they said, "You look great. Are you in love?" Yes, I'd reply. Because it is not what happened with those friendly, warm-blooded dolphins—but with a friendly, hot-blooded dolphin trainer named Dennis Aubrey. He was one of the senior dolphin and whale trainers at the aquarium. A former New York businessman who had grown up in Key Largo, Florida, Dennis had sold his successful business to pursue his childhood dreams which included buying a sailboat and becoming a dolphin trainer. The moment I laid eyes on him, the very instant we met, my heart did this sort of flip flop. Dennis made me nervous—women seemed to flock around him so I kept my distance. Despite that, every Wednesday we'd end up chatting and often working near each other. As the weeks passed, Dennis and I began flirting more and more. I never once thought about my old romance novel, *Lured into Dawn*—until the day Dennis pushed me into the dolphin pool. I was laughing so much that it wasn't until I climbed out and stood up that I realized he was staring at me. My clothes (not exactly a silk dress but a cotton Aquarium tee-shirt and shorts) clung to me a bit too provocatively for my comfort. I blushed beet red. Gee, I thought, this feels strangely familiar. That's when it hit me. *This was practically the opening scene in my very own book!*

Soon afterward, I came into the aquarium one morning to see Dennis, in the distance, surrounded by a group of young school kids. Very often classes would tour our marine mammal department as part of a school trip. As I stood there, watching him, he joked and chatted and laughed with the children. Gosh, I thought, he's so sweet and gentle. He'd make a great husband. Then it dawned on me: *I wrote this scene, too!*

Suffice to say, within the year we were engaged. In fact, our engagement party was actually at the New York Aquarium! A few weeks later, on a whim, we moved to Hawaii. That's when I found out that the fictional aquarium I had created for Richard Carson in Montego Bay wasn't fictional at all. The state of Hawaii had its own large marine life park called—you guessed it—Sea Life Park, Hawaii.

Three years after arriving in Hawaii, Dennis and I were married on the private island of Lana'i, home to a large group of Pacific Spinner dolphins. We lived on this small, rural island for almost four years, swimming sometimes daily with those magnificent wild dolphins. God had made my dream come true. I was living by the sea, with a man I deeply loved and admired, surrounded by my ocean family. And just like my romance novel, with God's continued blessing, we'll keep living happily ever after.

—Marcia Mager

The most beautiful summers take place in the Niagara region, and often the streets are filled with tourists and city folk. So it was nothing short of a miracle that it was a conscientious, kindhearted individual, rather than a careless, mean-spirited one, who found the lump in the road.

Brian was driving his truck down the familiar streets of his beloved hometown when he spotted something large lying in the middle of the road. Rather than swerve around it, as many motorists before him already had, he slowed his truck to take a closer look. When he reached the mysterious object, he saw that it was a woman's purse. *Probably left it on the hood of her car and unknowingly drove off,* he deduced.

Whoever the owner is, she must be frantic by now, Brian thought. He pulled his truck to the side of the road, dashed into the flow of traffic, and retrieved the purse. When he arrived home, he looked through the contents of the purse in the hope of finding the owner's identification. He found a wallet with a woman's name and phone number inside, and dialed the number. The woman on the other end was extremely thankful for his kind deed, and she asked if she could pick up her purse that evening. Brian politely offered to drop it off himself.

He returned the purse to the young woman, a student who attended the university in Saint Catherine's. Brian had deduced correctly: she had indeed left the purse on the hood of her car and driven off absentmindedly. She thanked Brian profusely and searched through the purse to see if anything was missing. Fortunately, even after the spill on the road, all the items were present except for her student ID card. She was a little disappointed that she had lost the identification she needed to take her exams, but still extremely grateful for the safe return of everything else. She thanked Brian again and said good-bye.

Several days later, Brian went to visit his brother Chris. As he walked up Chris's driveway, he noticed that his brother was talking with a young woman. As Brian approached the two, he realized that it was the owner of the purse—the same young woman he had seen days earlier. A look of confusion crossed his face, and the young woman looked equally confused.

Astonished to see her, he asked why she was at his brother's house. She in turn was dumbfounded to learn that Chris and Brian were brothers.

"Your brother just called me," she explained to Brian. "While he was driving his car down the highway this morning, he noticed something strange on the road. He stopped to retrieve it, and now I've come to pick it up."

Brian's brother had found her student card—the only missing item from the purse.

They all shared a laugh; she thanked the brothers again and left, all the original items in her purse now back and intact.

—*Katrina Ratz*

"Liz?" the slurred voice asked.

It was an early Wednesday morning in January 1999 and the officers of the J. Streicher Company, a securities lending firm on Wall Street, were bracing for a busy day.

Stockbroker Elizabeth Hartley, known to her friends as Liz, always had a phone glued to her ear at that time of day, sometimes fielding several phone calls at once. When the phone rang and she heard herself addressed by name, she was sure that the call was from a client. But as the caller continued to speak, Liz began to realize that something was wrong. The woman's speech was garbled and incoherent. *This woman is either loaded or stoned,* Liz thought. *And she's surely not a client.*

Who could it be?

Liz didn't hang up, because she had a relative in trouble. "Someone in my family was having problems at the time," she recalls, "and I assumed that it must be her. I didn't recognize the voice, but I thought Hey, when you're drunk or drugged you don't sound like yourself anyway." But after several minutes passed, Liz realized that it was a complete stranger, not a relative, who was on the other end of the line.

It's a wrong number, she thought, grasping the situation at last. *And this woman is in trouble!*

Liz frantically motioned a coworker, Emlyn Philbert, to her side and whispered: "I don't know what's going on here, but I think you should pick up the other phone and listen. What do you think we should do?"

Emlyn raced to the extension and eavesdropped on the conversation. From across the room she frantically mouthed a message to Liz: "We have to get her name and address. This sounds like an emergency!"

Meanwhile, the usually busy offices of J. Streicher were strangely quiet. The ordinary constant jangle of the telephones would surely have been distracting for the women, if not tempting. But on this particular morning the phones were uncharacteristically dead, giving the two stockbrokers the time and slack to talk to the stranger on the phone.

"Pretend you're the Liz she knows," Emlyn told her friend as she covered the phone with her hand. "If she realizes she has the wrong number, she may hang up. And then God knows what will happen."

"Nobody loves me. I just called to say good-bye," the stranger cried over the phone.

It was a delicate situation. The two stockbrokers desperately needed to extract information from the woman that could lead police to her home. But if the unknown "Liz" was a friend of the woman's, she wouldn't need to ask for such information. *How to identify the woman without making her unduly suspicious?*

"You know," Liz said ingenuously, "we have such a terrible connection, I can hardly hear you! Who is this? Your voice sounds so faint. Give me your number and I'll call you right back."

But 45 minutes went by before they succeeded in obtaining her number, and all the while the two women steadfastly kept the caller on the line.

"Sometimes all we heard was dead air," Liz remembers, "as the woman drifted in and out of consciousness. Emlyn—whom I call the queen of shmoozing—was just great. She wouldn't give up. She kept maintaining the conversation with the woman and didn't let her get off the phone."

Finally, the woman gave them a jumble of phone numbers. As Liz wrote them down, she frowned.

There are too many numbers here, she thought. Then consciousness dawned. Maybe three of those numbers were an area code!

Had the woman called long distance?

"She's calling from Hampton, Virginia!" she whispered a few minutes later to Emlyn. As Emlyn kept her talking on the other phone, Liz called the Hampton police.

And Emlyn was *still* talking to her when the squad car arrived at the scene.

The police officers pounded on the locked door, but got no response. Then they tried the windows, but they were shuttered tight.

Just then, a neighbor dashed out the door of an adjoining house and raced over to the men.

"I've got her key," she said breathlessly.

When the police entered the woman's bedroom, they found her lying on the bed, unconscious. Her night table was littered with vials of prescription drugs and bottles of alcohol. They were all empty.

The telephone receiver was gripped tight in her motionless hand.

An officer picked up the phone. Emlyn was still on the other end.

"Who are you?" he asked.

"We're the wrong number that she called!" the stockbroker replied.

In reflecting on the strange turn of events that led the two women to save the stranger's life four states away, Liz says: "It was just not her day to die! Everything conspired against it. First, she calls a Liz in Virginia and reaches instead a Liz in New York. Then the office strangely goes dead so we have the time and ability to help her. A neighbor appears on the porch with the key just in the nick of time. And finally, the woman falls unconscious just seconds before the police arrive! Talk about timing! . . . But what's most amazing of all to me is that she asked for *Liz*. You pay attention when someone calls you by your name. If she had called and asked for 'Chrissie' instead of 'Liz,' I would in all probability have just hung up, and that woman would surely be dead."

❧❧❧

Comment

In the celestial network of telephone systems, there are no wrong numbers.

*Josephine** had been blessed with two biological offspring of her own, but one day she told her husband Frank* that she wanted to adopt a child. She had just participated in a massive clothing drive that her church had sponsored for orphan children in China, and their plight moved her.

She wanted to do more than just send used clothing to Chinese orphanages, she said with emotion. Helping these abandoned and deprived children, she felt, meant reaching out in a very real and concrete way. And in Josephine's mind, the only way to truly make a difference in an orphan child's life was to adopt that child and bring him or her into the permanent sanctuary of her home. This was how she believed she could genuinely salvage a broken soul.

Fortunately, her husband was as idealistic as she and agreed to the plan. They contacted the right agencies, filled out the necessary paperwork, and traveled the great distance to China from their home in Canada to claim their child. From the mainland they journeyed to a small village where their child was housed, and it was many hours before they reached their final destination.

Upon their arrival at the orphanage—one of thousands scattered throughout the country—the fragile little boy who would soon be theirs was brought to meet them for the first time. As Josephine gazed at him tenderly, something about the child's appearance caught her eye. She gasped, and tears flowed down her cheeks. "This child was definitely meant to be ours," she told her husband with passion and certainty.

On the little feet of the tiny Chinese child were the shoes she had donated at the church clothing drive so many months before. She recognized them immediately and was sure whose they were, but just to be positive, she looked for his name on the inside of the shoe. The kindergarten teachers had asked the mothers to label all their children's belongings and articles of clothing in case they got lost.

The name of her biological son was still etched there in permanent ink.

The shoes had made their way to their new son before they had, and it seemed that they would further ease his transition into their home. For as he stepped over its threshold with those little shoes on his tiny feet, his hands would be held by parents convinced that this child was chosen to be theirs.

The long journey to his new parents' heart had already begun.

He was following in his brother's footsteps, all the way home.

—*Katrina Ratz*

Comment

Like clothing bound for summer camp, souls destined to enter each others lives are labeled with indelible spiritual ink.

"*We're* a very ordinary family," insists Suri Granek of Jerusalem, Israel. "The only difference between my family and others is that my children were not borne by me, but rather, for me. They were clearly meant to be ours. We really never needed proof that this was true, but an event that happened five years ago certainly validated our conviction that whoever came our way was destined to be part of our clan."

Despite her modest disclaimer, Suri's family—and its unusual composition—is extraordinary by most people's standards. And the event to which she refers was so singular and uncommon that it made national headlines in Israel.

The saga begins 27 years ago when Seymour Granek and Suri Fogel were married in New York City. "Throughout our engagement and the early years of our marriage," Suri remembers, "we talked about our mutual longing for a large family and agreed that the faster we got started on this enterprise, the better. Maybe it was already considered an unfashionable ambition for women of the seventies, but all I really wanted was the white picket fence and a warm, noisy, lively brood of kids."

Yet years passed, and the Graneks remained childless. Comprehensive examinations, painful procedures, myriad infertility treatments: all proved frustratingly fruitless. The legion of doctors whom the Graneks consulted remained clueless; none could determine the nature of the problem or even find anything wrong. Suri was ovulating normally and had a regular menstrual cycle; each doctor she saw promised that she would eventually get pregnant on her own. But she didn't.

"We waited for seven years before adopting," Suri recalls, "because every single doctor we saw was so positive that I would eventually conceive. We finally turned to the Louise Wise Agency in Manhattan, where we lived. Unlike so many other adoptive parents, who report tales of tribulation in the adoption process, ours went rather smoothly. We were blessed with a three-month-old, blonde-haired, blue-eyed cherub, whom we symbolically named Chaim (life) Simcha (joy). We felt that we would be able to give him a new life and that he in turn would bring us joy. The minute Chaim Simcha was placed in our arms, we knew: No matter how he had come to us, he was ours."

The Graneks adored their new child and relished the joys of parenting. After Chaim Simcha joined their family in November 1979, they reconsidered their earlier dreams. Maybe they couldn't have a large biological family—but what was to stop them from having a huge adoptive one instead?

Once again they turned to Louise Wise, but this time there was a long waiting list at the agency, and social workers gently pointed out that it would be unfair for the Graneks to adopt a second child when so many anxious couples were still waiting for their first.

"If you really want to adopt a second child," suggested one social worker, "why don't you consider a foreign-born child, or go abroad, for that matter?"

The Graneks were put in touch with a placement lawyer in Mexico. They started filing paperwork with both a Mexican adoption agency and the Immigration and Naturalization Service and were advised that the process would take at least six months.

"Astonishingly, it was only two months later [February 1982]," Suri recalls, "that we got a call from Mexico informing us that two babies were suddenly available . . . and each had to be picked up immediately.

"Christina*—a middle-aged woman who had applied to the same Mexican agency—flew with us from New York on the same plane, bound for the same emotional destination: a baby she could soon call her own.

"At the agency, we found the lawyer waiting, a baby cradled in each arm. He handed one baby to Christina, another to me.

" 'How did you decide which baby would be ours and which would be Christina's?' I asked, curious to know what criteria had influenced his choice.

" 'Oh, it didn't make any difference to me which baby I gave to whom,' " he said blithely. " 'It was random, really. Call it whimsy, impulse, arbitrary, whatever you like. Nothing specific guided my decision.' "

But when the Graneks glanced casually at the baby's birth certificate, they were shocked to discover that his birthdate—September 23—coincided with Suri's own. *They* were both born on the exact same date! Could it be that this particular baby was destined to be theirs and the lawyer's decision had not been arbitrary, after all? They named their dark-eyed, five-month-old Mexican baby Baruch after a deceased great-uncle and added the name Matityahu, which means "gift from God." For that's what Baruch was. . . .

The third baby to join the growing Granek family, in January 1983, was only five days old and was also of Mexican extraction. Unlike Baruch Matityahu, however, this baby seemed to have some Native American genes in her as well. She possessed strong Indian features, straight black hair, and dark skin. She was named Ahuva Leba, Hebrew for "love." The Graneks had it in abundance!

The rapidly expanding Granek family moved to Israel in September 1983, and there they adopted four-month-old Nava Yosefa, a Sabra (Israeli native) of Ethiopian extraction in July 1986 and Ariella Tzvia, a four-year-old Sabra in June 1989.

"Of all my children, it was always Baruch who was the healthiest and most active," muses Suri. "He was president of the student body of his school; a steady volunteer at the Jewish Institute for the Blind; and a star athlete. He excelled in all forms of sports. So it was ironic that of my five children, it was Baruch who became sick.

"In 1995, a few short months after his bar mitzvah, Baruch began complaining of severe leg cramps that were very painful and disrupted his sleep.

"I took him to the local doctor, who checked him out thoroughly but could find nothing wrong. He suspected 'growing pains' but told us to come back if the pains intensified. 'Don't worry,' he said!"

Over time, however, the severity and frequency of the cramps increased. The second visit to the doctor netted tests and a referral to Bikur Cholim Hospital in Jerusalem, where more tests were run. It was there that the grim diagnosis was handed down by nephrologist Dr. Avi Katz.

"Baruch's kidney function is about 10 percent right now. His potassium levels are sky high. It's probably premature for me to say this, but I think that further analysis will reveal what I've already unhappily concluded: Baruch is suffering from chronic and irreversible kidney disease."

The doctor's suspicions were, sadly, well-founded. Not just one, but both of Baruch's kidneys were severely damaged. Physicians treated his condition with several different medications, monitored him constantly, and took his blood pressure several times a day. "You can anticipate his condition being stable for at least a year before he experiences a decline," they told the Graneks.

But they were wrong.

Within only a few short weeks, Baruch had deteriorated rapidly, far in advance of the doctors' timetable. He had become severely anemic, weak, and infirm, and was too frail even to leave his bed. What had become of the strong, healthy, athletic boy Baruch was just a few weeks before? Suri wondered. He had vanished, and a pale wisp of a boy had taken his place.

Two months after the original diagnosis, Baruch had the first of an ongoing series of operations, procedures that initially helped but later failed him, each and every time.

Over a short period of time, the once-robust Baruch had become skeletal, an unrecognizable shadow of his former self. Different methods, multitudinous surgical procedures—including several insertions of temporary and emergency shunts—were attempted time and time again, but each was beset by complications. Finally, the doctor used the word that had hovered in the family's thoughts for so long . . . the word that simultaneously held promise and hope . . . the word that no one had dared breathe, for its enormity was too much to contemplate . . . the word "transplant."

"I want to give Baruch my kidney," Suri told the doctor. "Let me be the first one to be tested as a possible match," she begged.

The doctor stared at Suri. He was familiar with the unusual composition of her family and knew that Baruch was adopted.

What were the chances of Suri—an American of European descent—being a match for a Mexican?

"Forget about it," the doctor advised. "The odds are strong against any pair that is not genetically or ethnically linked in some significant way."

But Suri was not to be dissuaded. If anything, she was known to be a persistent type who believed in following her heart's journey. The unusual family she and Seymour had assembled and loved fervently was certainly testimony to that.

"You'd be wasting your time to even get tested," the doctor said. "Suri," he lectured her, "let me tell you what odds you're facing. You need to fulfill three criteria in order to be considered a viable kidney donor. First, your blood type has to be compatible with the recipient's; second, you must share common antigens; and third, the recipient can't have antibodies that would reject the donor's kidneys. As an adoptive mother, your chances are about nil."

"Let me at least test to see what blood type I am," Suri said stubbornly.

At the lab, the technician glanced sympathetically at Suri as she gave her the news. "I know you're testing for compatibility with your son," she said compassionately. "I'm sorry to tell you that you have a rare blood type—B positive—which only 8 percent of the world's population has. I know how depressing the news must be."

But Suri was, much to the technician's surprise, elated instead. "This is the best news!" she shouted jubilantly. "Baruch is also blood type B positive!"

Heartened by the wonderful coincidence, Suri then bombarded the doctor with pleas to be tissue-typed— the test where compatibility between donor and recipient almost always resides in their sharing a common genetic heritage.

It was not that the doctor wasn't supportive or understanding of Suri's enormous drive to give the gift of life to her son. It was precisely because he was so sensitive to the pain and trauma that Suri had undergone that he did not want her to suffer any further. He wanted to spare her the disappointment of not being able to literally give of herself to her son.

"Listen," he told Suri, "it's quite a surprise that you and Baruch share the same blood type, but the statistics indicate that 8 percent of the population do. But statistics also reveal that your chances of sharing common antigens are about zero. The whole thing's impossible."

"It doesn't hurt to try," Suri reasoned. The doctor threw up his hands in surrender, and she proceeded with the tissue-typing test.

Waiting at the nephrologist's office several weeks later for the test results to come in finally, Suri paced the floor nervously. Every minute seemed like an hour, every hour an eternity, as she felt her son's life hang in the balance. Then the phone rang and she overhead the following conversation between two secretaries on the speakerphone.

"Great news, they have half of their antigens in common," the lab secretary reported to the nephrologist's assistant, who sat stunned in her seat.

"I'm shocked," she told her colleague over the phone.

"Why are you so shocked?" the lab secretary asked, puzzled. "After all, she's his MOTHER, isn't she?"

"You don't understand," the nephrologist's secretary responded. "She's his *adoptive* mother. She's an American Jew of European descent. He's a Mexican American. They share no common genetic link."

Baruch's antibodies also proved compatible with Suri's. So, on all three counts—blood type, shared antigens, and compatible antibodies—adoptive mother and adoptive son were a perfect match!

But Baruch didn't want to take his mother's kidney. He felt that it was too great a sacrifice. He had heard that kidney transplants are exceedingly painful procedures, especially for the donor.

"It's going to hurt you!" he protested to Suri.

"Baruch," Suri replied, "the emotional pain of watching you suffer is far greater than any physical pain I would ever have to endure."

The successful transplant took place exactly nine months after the original diagnosis. Suri feels that the number is laden with meaning.

"Baruch was a brand-new person immediately after the transplant," she says. "I felt as if he had been reborn."

The date of the transplant also held special significance for her. "The transplant took place on the [Hebrew date] 18th of Tishrei," she remembers. In Hebrew, 18 means chai—life.

Baruch is now 18 years old, has just graduated from high school, and, as a result of his medical history, plans to become a doctor so that he may help others as he was helped.

"Today," Suri says proudly, "Baruch is healthy, muscular, physically fit, and, altogether, doing beautifully. Although he has had to give up his beloved soccer because the kidney was transplanted in his abdomen (a vulnerable place for soccer players), he continues to shine as a basketball star."

Suri recalls with wonder the day the Mexican lawyer placed the infant Baruch in her arms, his action seemingly dictated by sheer whim.

What if he had been placed in Christina's arms instead? What were the chances that Christina would also be a compatible donor? Would Baruch even be alive today if Christina had been arbitrarily chosen as his adoptive mother, and not Suri?

Suri is awestruck by the miracle of their perfect match, but modestly discounts her own role in literally saving Baruch's life.

"These are my children," she says simply. "The only difference is that they didn't grow inside of me. They grew inside my heart, instead."

༚༚

Comment
The unbreakable bond between mother and child can transcend birth, death, and apparent cosmic error.

S*everal* decades ago, Lillian Miller was an energetic, spirited, fearless young woman who loved driving long distances, did not tire easily, and relished any opportunity to do a good deed. This unusual combination of characteristics meant that she was frequently asked to perform favors for people.

Because of her good-naturedness, she was enlisted to drive two young servicemen to Fort Sill, Oklahoma, from her hometown of New Castle, Pennsylvania. Having faithfully fulfilled her mission and dropped the men on base, she turned her car around and immediately started back home. Speeding down the highway, though, Lillian had second thoughts.

"Now, you're not being very realistic," she chastised herself. "You have a good 18-hour trip ahead of you. Better fill up on some coffee first."

She spotted a little diner off the highway, ablaze with light. She pulled in. Grabbing her thermos from the car, she went inside and asked the waitress to fill it to the top. She also ordered a separate cup to sip while she sat waiting at the counter. She was drinking her coffee, lost in thought, when a plaintive voice broke her reverie.

A few seats down from her, a young serviceman in uniform sat quietly weeping. A waitress hovered over him, anxiously trying to soothe him with words of comfort, but nothing she said seemed to help. Lillian listened intently.

"It's my first child and I want to be there for my wife," he said. "I can't believe I'm going to miss the birth of my baby!"

"Are you sure it's not false labor?" the waitress asked.

"She just called from the hospital. The doctor is sure she's in the early stages of labor. It might be a while, he says, since it's the first, but the baby is definitely on its way."

"I can't believe you have no way to get home," the waitress said sympathetically.

"There is no plane service from here to Akron, and the next bus and train out don't leave until tomorrow. . . . Tomorrow will probably be too late!"

"Excuse me," Lillian said. She stood up and approached the serviceman. "I'm sorry, but I couldn't help but overhear your conversation. Did you say that you have to get to Akron, as in Akron, Ohio?"

"That's right," he said. He looked up at her in puzzlement, wondering where she was going with this.

"Well, this is a mighty interesting coincidence . . . ," she said, smiling. "I'm headed towards New Castle, Pennsylvania, which is about an hour and a half away from Akron. I can drive you to New Castle, and then you can try to get a hitch from there to Akron. I'll be glad to give you a lift."

"This is unbelievable!" the serviceman exclaimed. "You are so kind. Please . . . let me pay you for the trip."

"Oh, absolutely not," Lillian said. "I'm driving to New Castle anyway. I'm glad to help you out. Hop in."

All through the trip, the serviceman kept reiterating his joy, his gratitude, his appreciation, his insistence that Lillian allow him to pay for the gas, the tolls, the trip itself—but Lillian was more obstinate than he.

"Save your money for the baby," she advised. "I told you . . . I was going to New Castle anyway."

But when they reached Lillian's hometown and she turned around to tell the serviceman—who had stretched out on the back seat to catch a few winks—that they had arrived, her expression softened. He was fast asleep, and he looked so young and vulnerable and sweet. *His first baby*, he had said. *What if he couldn't find a hitch from New Castle to Akron, after all? Having come such a long way, how would he feel if he missed the momentous event of his baby's birth?*

In a split second, she decided. She wouldn't wake the serviceman and tell him they were in New Castle. She would extend herself and drive him all the way to the hospital in Akron. "For me," she reasoned, "it's just three hours out of my way. For him, it's a lifetime."

When they reached Akron, Lillian gently roused him and told him where they were. Startled, he gazed at her, overwhelmed by her kindness. "You've really gone out on a limb for me," he said. "How can I ever repay you? Please give me your name and address, so I can send you something as a token of my appreciation."

But Lillian was a stubborn sort.

"You'll do no such thing," she commanded him sternly. You'll need every penny you have for all your baby's needs, wait and see. . . . I'm delighted I was able to help you out, and good luck to you. Bye." Lillian waved one final time and quickly drove away.

But not back home to New Castle, after all. It was another hour-and-a-half trip, and even the tireless Lillian had finally become weary and spent. It was three o'clock in the morning, and what she needed more than anything else right now was . . . a bed.

"I know!" she decided spontaneously. "I'll go to Dorothy's and sleep there."

Dorothy, her sister, lived in a trailer park in Kent, about 10 miles from Akron. Even though it was the middle of the night, she knew she was welcome at her sister's anytime. Her sister would throw open the door, smile at her warmly, and excitedly usher her inside.

But when she arrived at the trailer and pounded insistently at the door, no one answered. "That's strange," Lillian muttered. "Dorothy's not a heavy sleeper . . ."

She went around to the bedroom window and hammered on it loudly. She waited expectantly for the figure of her sister to peer out the window or be framed in the kitchen doorway. Or, if not her sister, then at least her grandmother Lucille, or her niece Debbie, or Eddie, . . . But no one, not a single member of the family, stirred at all.

Lillian ran back to the trailer door and knocked noisily once more. Still no response from inside. But she had managed to awaken the next-door neighbor. "Is something wrong?" he called out to her as he emerged from his trailer, clad only in pajamas.

It was then that she smelled gas.

She motioned to him wildly. "I think something's the matter with my sister and her family. . . . I can't wake them up, and I think I smell gas. . . . Could you come here and tell me if you smell it too?"

The neighbor ran over and sniffed. "Smells like gas to me," he said, alarmed. "Let me get some tools from my car."

He raced back and pried open Dorothy's trailer door with a tire iron. As the two entered, they were engulfed by heavy gas fumes and began choking. Lillian found the limp, dazed figures of her family members strewn around the bedrooms, and she and the neighbor pulled them out of the trailer into the brisk fresh air. Thankfully, every single one of them survived.

Decades later, Lillian Miller still feels touched by grace; the episode remains one of the defining moments of her life.

"If I hadn't picked up the serviceman in Oklahoma and driven him all the way to Akron, my family might very well have died that night. Sometimes, when you're performing an act of kindness, the person who ends up benefiting the most is yourself!"

ം♦ം

Comment
How far can an act of kindness spread? From this end of the earth to the other and back to our very own front door.

*T*he year is 1942, and a 17-year-old girl, just recently graduated from Waycross High, heads to Jacksonville, Florida. It's the war years and there are jobs to be had in our big-city neighbor to the south. Jeanette Eunice is on her way.

She lives with her sister, and one Sunday afternoon in June of '42 they go for a stroll downtown. They look in the shop windows, they stop by Confederate Park, and then they duck into a small café just next to the park.

Enter Al Sandor, a young Marine from Scranton, Pennsylvania, two years her senior. He captures the young girl's heart. She captures his heart.

They date throughout that summer, whenever he can get away from his training at the Naval Air Station, and they get along right nicely. Sometimes Jeanette will ride home to Waycross on the Greyhound bus for a weekend visit with her parents. Frequently, and more and more frequently, young Sandor will take the bus up on Sunday morning just so they can ride back to Jacksonville together on the return journey. But World War II, like all wars before it, has a way of sticking its big way into romance.

Al is transferred, first to San Diego, then to the Pacific, to Guadalcanal. The battles are a long way from home, but he's not alone; he's got Jeanette's prom picture with him, and he carries it into every battle.

The war drags on. They write, and one day he returns on leave, but he has to visit his family, now working for the war effort in Detroit. Then it's back to the Pacific, this time the Marshall Islands.

Finally comes the day when our young Marine is discharged. What does he do? He comes immediately back to Jacksonville to see the Waycross girl he left behind.

They visit for three days, and when he returns to Detroit they begin writing those love letters that everyone in the whole wide world should have the opportunity to write at some point in his or her life.

But it's still the war years. People are coming and going. Upheaval comes to everyone.

The space between the letters gets longer and longer, longer and longer, until eventually they stop.

"I thought, '*Jeanette, that boy's never coming back.* You'd better get on with your life,' " she recalls.

Jeanette marries, and she writes him a letter telling him so. It takes him seven years to get over her "Dear John" letter, but finally he, too, marries. They raise their families. Unbeknownst to both of them they both raise five children. Jeanette's husband dies in 1976.

Fast forward 54 years, to October 12, 1996. A widow sits alone on another Sunday afternoon. She finds herself going through old memorabilia. She's known to her friends as a pack rat. It's time to clean out the files.

There, on a bit of yellowed paper half crumpled and jagged with age, she finds a name and an address.

"It was a page out of one of those 10-cent autograph books I bought at Kress's for graduation from high school," Jeanette recalls. "I've carried that book around with me for more than fifty years. I had torn the page out because, after all, I got married and I didn't think my husband would appreciate my keeping that address. I was surprised when, on that Sunday afternoon, I found that page again in a stack of old papers. Al had signed it before he left to go to the Pacific way back in '42."

It was all she had.

Three times she throws it into the trash can. Three times she picks it out again.

The third time's the charm.

"I tried to say, 'That's past. Leave it alone.' But I couldn't leave it. I looked at that little piece of paper and I said, 'Let the chips fall where they may. I'm going to call. If his wife answers I'll just tell her I'm an old friend and we'll have some laughs about the old days.' "

But there is no wife to answer, she having died three years earlier. Instead, an older son picks up the phone. More importantly, he takes the message.

An excited Al Sandor returns her call, but she's too afraid to pick up the receiver. Instead she lets the answering machine record a voice she hasn't heard in five decades. Then she listens to the message, again and again, until the tape wears out.

Then, late that night, she returns his call.

Once unleashed, how the current flows again between these two. They burn up the phone lines and boost the stock of Southern Bell, talking like two teenagers into the night.

"I tell her, 'The first time I picked you out. The second time you picked me out—of the trash can,' " says Al.

Added to these phone calls are the wonderful letters, missives that begin, "Hello Darling . . ." and end, "All My Love."

There's a short visit in December and another one in February. Then two weeks later Al returns to Waycross and he's been here ever since. He has to stay. There's a wedding next Saturday he'll attend.

Yep, 55 years after he and Jeanette met in that little café in Jacksonville, the pair celebrated their love supreme with a wedding at 2 P.M. at St. Joseph's Catholic Church, Saturday, May 17, 1997. At the ages of 72 and 74, respectively, Jeanette Eunice Thrift and Al Sandor picked up right where they left off.

"Some things just seem fated to be, and that's all there is to that," says Jeanette.

In the time leading up to their reunion, both parties, a thousand miles apart, knew something was going on.

"I sat there in my chair a month before Jeanette called me," Al says. "I had kept a picture of her with me all those years down in my things in my basement. For some reason I found myself looking at that photo again and telling myself, 'Jeanette Eunice, I'd sure like to see you again.' A month later, her call came through. I was surprised and I wasn't surprised all at the same time."

The same thing was going on with Jeanette.

"I remember telling someone about that time, 'Sue, there's something going on in my life. I can't put my finger on it, but something's going to happen.' One month later, I came across that address again," says Jeanette.

She found the address, but it was an out-of-date address.

"I picked up the phone and called information for Detroit, Michigan. The operator said they didn't have an 'Al Sandor' listed, but I used to work for the telephone company and I asked her to check the outlying areas. There he was. I'll forever be thankful for that operator."

That airport reunion in Jacksonville in December was some kind of emotional time.

"We're still on cloud nine. I thought I'd be the one to cry, but he started crying," says Jeanette. "Although both of us loved our spouses and raised good families, I think both of us unconsciously had the other in mind all our lives. I know I had never forgotten him. In fact, he became my yardstick by which I measured all the boys I knew. He was always the perfect gentleman with me."

"She was an innocent country girl from South Georgia," says Al. "And I left her that way. From the moment I first saw her, she's been my shining star."

What did they do for an exciting date back in those wartime Jacksonville days?

"We used to listen to the Grand Old Opry," says Al, a lifelong country music fan. "And we still listen to the Grand Old Opry."

"You know, I still have to pinch myself sometimes," admits Jeanette. "I was talking to him across the kitchen table the other day and I said, 'Here I am. I can't believe I'm talking to Al Sandor.'"

After all this you won't get an argument from these two about that great chess master in the sky, moving all the pieces around. And you won't get an argument about the overwhelming, timeless power of love. A love supreme.

—Larry Purdom

*I*t was December 23rd. My children and I lived in a tiny house. Being a single mom, going to college, and supporting my children completely alone, Christmas looked bleak. As I looked around me, realization dawned with a slow, twisting pain. We were poor.

Our tiny house had two bedrooms, both off the living room. They were so small that my baby daughter's crib barely fit into one, and my son's twin bed and dresser into the other. There was no way they could share a room, so I made my bed every night on the living room floor. The three of us shared the only closet in the house. We were snug, always only a few feet from each other, day and night. With no doors on the children's rooms, I could see and hear them at all times. It made them feel secure and made me feel close to them—a benefit I would not have had in other circumstances.

It was late, almost eleven. The snow was falling softly, silently. I was wrapped in a blanket, sitting at the window watching the powdery flakes flutter in the moonlight, when my front door vibrated against a pounding fist. Alarmed, I wondered who would be at my home so late on a snowy winter night. I opened the door to find several strangers grinning from ear to ear, their arms laden with boxes and bags. Confused, but finding their joyous spirit contagious, I grinned right back.

"Are you Susan?" The man stepped forward as he sort of pushed a box at me.

Nodding stupidly, unable to find my voice, I was sure they thought I was mentally deficient.

"These are for you." The woman thrust another box at me with a huge, beaming smile. The porch light and the snow falling behind her cast a glow on her dark hair, lending her an angelic appearance. I looked down into her box. It was filled with treats, a fat turkey, and all the makings of a traditional Christmas dinner. My eyes filled with tears as the realization of what they were there for washed over me.

Finally coming to my senses, I invited them in. Following the husband were two children, staggering with the weight of their gifts for my little family. This wonderful, beautiful family, who were total strangers to me, somehow knew exactly what we needed. They brought wrapped gifts for each of us, a full buffet for me to make on Christmas, and many "extras" that I could never afford. Visions of a beautiful, "normal" Christmas literally danced in my head. Somehow my secret wish for Christmas was materializing right in front of me.

My mysterious angels then handed me an envelope, giving me another round of grins, and each of them hugged me. They wished me a Merry Christmas and disappeared into the night as suddenly as they had appeared. The whole experience seemed to have lasted for hours, yet it was over in less than a couple of minutes.

Amazed and deeply touched, I looked around me at the boxes and gifts strewn at my feet and felt the ache of depression suddenly being transformed into a childlike joy. I began to cry. I cried hard, sobbing tears of the deepest gratitude. A great sense of peace filled me. The knowledge of God's love reaching into my tiny corner of the world enveloped me like a warm quilt. My heart was full. I dropped to my knees amid all the boxes and offered a heartfelt prayer of thanks.

Suddenly I remembered the envelope. Like a child I ripped it open and gasped at what I saw. A shower of bills flitted to the floor. Gathering them up, I began to count the five-, ten-, and twenty-dollar bills. My vision blurred with tears, I counted the money, then counted it again to make sure I had it right. Now sobbing, I said it out loud. "One hundred dollars."

There was no way the visitors could have known it, but I had just received a disconnect notice from the gas company. I simply didn't have the money needed and feared my family would be without heat by Christmas. The envelope of cash would give us warmth and a tree for Christmas. Suddenly, we had all we needed and more.

It is now several years since our Christmas angels visited. I have since remarried, and we are happy and richly blessed. Every year since that Christmas in

1993, we have chosen a family less blessed than we are. We bring them carefully selected gifts, food, and treats, and as much money as we can spare. It's our way of passing on what was given to us. It is the "ripple effect" in motion. We hope that the cycle continues and that some day, the families that we share with will also pass it on.

—*Susan Fahncke*

I was excited to meet Sandi. My editor had said we were kindred spirits, and from the moment we started to correspond, we both knew that she was right. Sandi was a graphic artist and calligrapher. Her work was bright, colorful, and playful, especially her well-known "trademark"—a little angel named Ariane whom she drew and put on bookmarks. She liked to present these bookmarks to people as little gifts, usually with the saying "Miracles happen to those who believe!" inscribed below the drawing. A woman after my own heart!

Sandi and I wanted to meet in person, but it seemed impossible, since I live in North Dakota and she in Massachusetts. On a whim, I wrote to tell her that my family and I would be vacationing on Martha's Vineyard in July, and I had one day when I knew I would be free. Curiously, she said that she was going to be visiting her parents on Cape Cod that very same day. I offered to ferry over from the island, and she asked if her mother could join us for the fun of it.

In spite of the warmth of our previous exchanges, I admit that I was nervous about meeting someone who was basically still a stranger. Although the sound of the ferry engine and the rhythm of the sea usually calm me, I found myself reaching in my bookbag for a small volume I had brought with me, *Peace Is Every Step* by the Vietnamese Buddhist monk Thich Nhat Hanh. The book was little known by others, but well loved by me. It contained a meditation that I found very soothing: "Breathing in, I calm my body. Breathing out, I smile. Dwelling in the present moment, I know this is a wonderful moment." I closed my eyes, reciting it over and over as the ferry cut through the Sound.

Sandi and her mother turned out to be delightful, and the afternoon started to slip away more quickly than any of us wanted it to. I felt comfortable with both of them, and judging from their smiles and enthusiasm, they felt the same about me.

"I have to admit something," Sandi said gently. "I was both excited and nervous about meeting you, so on my way over here, I was reading this wonderful little book called *Peace Is Every Step*. It has this one breathing exercise I really like." She recited just the one I had used during the ferry ride.

My jaw must have dropped, because they both looked at me with alarmed faces and said "What's wrong?" simultaneously.

I silently reached in my bookbag and showed them my book. They gasped.

From the first letter, Sandi and I had sensed that we would be friends. From that moment on, we knew we were soul mates, too.

—*Robin Silverman*

❦

Comment

Kindred spirits often drink at the same fountain of wisdom.

*I*n the mid-sixties, I moved to a new town where everyone was a stranger and I had not yet made new friends. I had just broken up with the man I was dating, and I felt desperately lonely. To compound my emotional travail, I came down with the flu and was too sick to drag myself to the local doctor. There was no one around whom I could ask to drive me to his office, run an errand to the pharmacy, pick up some groceries, cook chicken soup, or, in general, give me much-needed nurturing. I felt utterly bereft and totally alone.

Feeling that there was not a single soul in the world who cared about me, I decided to "end it all." I got out of bed and hunted for the gun I kept in a drawer. Just as I was raising it to my temple, the telephone rang. It startled me and caused me to jump. I picked up the receiver and it was the man I had just broken up with. When I heard his voice on the other end, I didn't say anything, but just started crying. Hearing my sobs, he yelled: "I'll be there in 10 minutes!" He arrived shortly and told me how he happened to call at this particular time.

He had been driving down a street in a neighboring city when he seemed to feel something hit him on the back of the head, and he thought he heard a voice say, "Stop! Call Loree!" The shock caused him to hit the brake, and when he slid to a stop he found himself directly in front of a telephone booth. He jumped out of the car and called me. It was that telephone call that saved my life!

Several years later, now happily married and doing well, I had a sudden strong feeling one day that I should call my youngest brother, with whom I had only sporadic contact. Since we were not close, I didn't immediately act on my emotions, but all day long the nagging feeling would not go away. Unable to shake it off, I finally approached my husband and told him about my strange "message."

"What should I do?" I asked him.

"Call him!" he said.

I didn't even know whether I had my brother's current phone number, but I rummaged through various drawers until I found it. When I finally reached him, his response to my call was strange and bizarre.

"You don't know what you've done!" he simply cried over and over again. "You don't know what you've done."

I tried to find out what he meant by this mysterious remark, but he refused to elaborate. As much as I tried, I could not pry any further information from him. He just kept reiterating this one sentence, over and over again. Finally, I gave up and bade him good night, and gently hung up the phone.

A few weeks later I made the 500-mile trip home and went to visit him.

"What did you mean when you said on the phone that I didn't know what I'd done?" I finally asked.

He mutely pointed to the ceiling and I saw the bullet lodged there.

He told me that he had been on the brink of despair and about to "end it all" when I called. He actually had the gun raised to his temple and was about to pull the trigger, when the ringing of the telephone startled him, as it had me so many lifetimes ago. His hand jerked and the shot went into the ceiling instead of through his head. This time, *I* had been the one to follow my intuition and act on an impulse, and my brother's life had been saved as a result, just as mine had been so many years before.

—*Loree Brown*

Comment
So powerful is the force that words of caring possess, they can help to alter the trajectory of a speeding bullet and resurrect a human life.

A cry in the night from my two-year-old daughter jolted me awake for the third night in a row. As I entered her room, Marissa was sitting on her bed, holding her head and crying. Between sobs, she repeatedly told me that her head was "ouchie."

I was beginning to doubt the assumption I had made several days earlier. Life in our house had been hectic. I had recently opened my own business and was busy preparing for a new baby to arrive in six weeks. Our two girls were also adapting to having a sitter all day while Mommy was working. It was enough to make a 30-year-old feel like crying and holding her head, too. I had naturally assumed that Marissa was just craving a little attention. Now, however, I was worried.

The next morning and throughout the day, Marissa continued to complain about her head. Her medical checkup was only a few days away, but I decided that I would call the doctor to discuss my concern. The nurse suggested that if the headaches continued, I should mention them to the doctor during Marissa's checkup.

On February 6, 1997, I explained the situation to the doctor. As I watched him proceed with his examination, I became concerned as he performed simple reflex tests on Marissa's toes not once or twice but several times. He also seemed to spend a great deal of time shining a light in her eyes. A few minutes later, I sat and listened. The doctor explained that headaches in two-year-olds were not very common. Given this fact, coupled with some poor reflex response during Marissa's exam, he wanted to do some tests to rule out anything more serious—including a brain tumor. *Just being cautious,* he assured me. The MRI procedure that he was requesting would essentially allow the doctors a peek inside her brain. "Brain tumors in children are very rare," he repeated.

After arriving home and calling my husband, David, I immediately called Marissa's grandma, Barb. "Stepmother" never seemed to convey the warmth of the special relationship that Barb and I shared. I was only 14 when my mother passed away. Looking back, I am impressed at how my father raised three teenage girls alone through the next six years. Although I still longed for my mother, I was a little unsure when my dad remarried in 1987. We'd have to share him with Barb and her two children.

But over the years I discovered a special kind of relationship with Barb. I now had a special mom to do things with, to help plan my wedding, to rush to the hospital when I gave birth, and to love my children as her own grandchildren. I had someone I could talk to about my own mother, someone to share special occasions, and someone to watch over my father. During this difficult time with Marissa, Barb did much to encourage and support me, even though she was dealing with her own bad headache from a sinus infection.

The next week, the strain of waiting for the MRI appointment, fear of the unknown, the daily stress of caring for two little ones, coupled with the raging hormones of pregnancy caused me to crumple one afternoon. I found myself sobbing on the phone to Barb. She, of course, rushed to my house and sat with me and helped to pass the time. She spent some time rocking Marissa and reading to both girls. As the girls napped, Barb told me how hard she had been praying that everything would be fine. The possibility of a brain tumor was unthinkable to her. Marissa had not yet lived, Barb said. Then Barb told me she had prayed that if someone were to have a brain tumor, it should be her, not Marissa. She had lived a life full of love, marriage, children, and grandchildren.

On February 20, my father and Barb sat together in the waiting room at Children's Hospital as the staff began to prepare Marissa for her MRI. She was difficult to put to sleep, but finally, with an IV, she was asleep, and the procedure began. David stayed in the room with her, but because of my pregnancy, I stayed in the waiting room, where Dad and Barb continued to assure me that things would be fine.

The next morning our doctor telephoned with the results. I could hear his relief when he told me that the MRI did not show a brain tumor or anything else serious. The MRI did, however, show that Marissa had a severe sinus infection. At her age that would account for the headaches and perhaps for the coordination problems. The good news was that with three weeks of dosing with antibiotic "pink stuff," the headaches would disappear.

Life in our home seemed to return to normal as we prepared for the arrival of our third child in March. As usual, Dad and Barb met us at the hospital for the birth of our son, Thomas. After that, I thought things would finally settle down.

Our annual Easter gathering and Easter egg hunt was held at Dad and Barb's house. Barb was very carefree, but Dad seemed very tense. Something just did not seem right. The whole atmosphere that day was very stressful. Almost immediately after my sisters and I returned to our own homes, we phoned one another to try to figure out what was so terribly wrong. We all agreed that Barb and Dad were both acting strange. The following Monday, Dad asked if we had noticed anything different about Barb. She was not acting normally. It started with little things, like randomly changing the channel on the television, but included more serious incidents like shopping excessively. She was also complaining of a constant throbbing sinus headache.

Their family physician dismissed it all as some sort of depression and prescribed an antidepressant, but the next week things escalated. The odd little behaviors became more bizarre. Dad took her to the doctor who was treating her diabetes rather than returning to the family physician. The doctor immediately sent her to the hospital for further testing.

I remember sitting with Barb at the hospital as the neurologist gave her a short, simple test. What day was it? What hospital was she in? What floor was she on? Why was she here? Could she remember the following items: cat, book, chair? Somehow I found the strength not to cry in front of Barb when I saw that she couldn't pass the test. I knew in my heart that something was terribly wrong. Like a child, I suddenly wanted to run away to the playground for a place to hide and cry, as I had done almost 16 years earlier when my mother had died.

The next day, after an MRI, the doctors made the diagnosis. Barb had a massive brain tumor. The doctors figured that it might have started growing sometime in January when her "sinus headaches" began. By now, it was very large and would require surgery at the minimum. But Barb did not make it to surgery, because the tumor hemorrhaged. My special mom, Barbara Vork Barth, died on April 12, 1997, less than one week after being diagnosed with a brain tumor.

Were the similarities in condition and timing between Barb and Marissa a mere coincidence? Or are there a handful of souls on earth so angelic that they would literally give up their life for someone they love? I believe my heart knows the miracle in our story, but in either case I am grateful for the rare opportunity to have been loved so deeply by two mothers and to have witnessed their courage and commitment to their families.

Although our girls were only four and two when their grandma died, their love for her was strong. The headaches in the night no longer wake Marissa and no longer frighten me. My new challenge is to remember the example of strength and love as I wipe away my daughters' tears and comfort them as they cry for their grandma.

—Jill E. Reed

*W*as it bad timing, bad luck, or something else?

Colleen Jacobsen didn't even know that her checkbook had been stolen until she was handed one of her checks — *with a forged signature* — to cash.

Out of 36 banks in Lancaster, Pennsylvania, the brazen thief had made the fatal mistake of trying to cash the stolen check at the very institution where the rightful owner worked — *as a teller.*

And it was precisely this teller's window that the perpetrator randomly approached to make the transaction.

Hey, this is my check! Colleen thought, her eyes widening in disbelief, as she noted her own name and address printed at the top. She had recently ordered new checks, and now, it seemed, one of them had somehow come into the possession of the very woman standing in front of her . . . face to face!

Thinking quickly, Colleen tried to stall the thief while she motioned quietly to a coworker nearby. The coworker alerted a bank security officer and simultaneously put in a call to the police.

While she waited for the police to arrive, Colleen kept making small talk.

"So . . . where'd you get the check?" she asked the thief casually.

The thief told her that a woman had given it to her so that she could buy some clothes. "The woman is right outside . . . do you want to talk to her?" the thief asked, apparently growing nervous.

"Yes, I would."

The thief wheeled around and walked out the door. She didn't come back.

Although some of the bank staff followed, the woman was faster on her feet than they, and she disappeared in a flash.

But a security guard working for a neighboring company heard the commotion, spotted the woman, and joined in the chase. As the thief ducked into an alleyway, she hurled a pad of personal checks into the street. She was then wrestled to the ground by the security officer and two other men and held until the police arrived.

In reconstructing the robbery, police concluded that the new checkbooks had been delivered to Colleen's house earlier that morning, when she was already on her way to work. Because the box of checks would not fit into the mail slot, the mail carrier had left the package outside Colleen's door, making it an easy target for thieves to snatch.

"It's amazing," Lancaster police officer Don Erb said. "What are the odds? Colleen normally rotates between different branches of the bank and just happened to be working at that branch for that week only, and the thief just happened to come into that branch and just happened to go to her window."

"How can you top that?"

The incident took place at the First Union Queen Street Branch on March 30, 2000.

Colleen had just come on duty a few minutes before the thief walked in the door.

I'm getting more and more absentminded by the day, I berated myself, as I struggled to find the change I needed to buy a subway token for my trip home.

It was true. As I advanced headlong into middle age, my forgetfulness was becoming increasingly more pronounced, precipitating all kinds of little crises and minor disasters.

How did I manage to travel to Manhattan without my wallet in my purse? I wondered. *Had I found spare change at the bottom of my bag to buy my subway token in Brooklyn?* Well, if I had, there wasn't any left. Bad news: with no wallet in my purse and with no welcome jangle of loose coins coming from deep inside, I found myself vacillating between laughter and despair. Imagine: a middle-class woman from a comfortable home who lacks $1.50 to get back home!

It wasn't a tragedy or an emergency, but in that moment I felt vulnerable and lost. I didn't travel to Manhattan often and didn't know my way around the city. I had no friends or acquaintances in the vicinity and couldn't think of anyone who worked in the surrounding area. So what was I to do?

I hunted again in my purse, hoping that I had somehow overlooked a nook or cranny where that seemingly insignificant but all-important sum might hide. Oh, to have $1.50 in my hand! I looked wistfully at the commuters rushing by, longing for a familiar face to suddenly appear. I felt invisible and helpless as people whizzed by without giving me so much as a glance. What should I do?

Well, I told myself, *you could throw yourself on the mercy of the token booth clerk and beg her to let you through the turnstile.*

Or you could find a policeman and ask him for $1.50.

But I couldn't do either of those things. I felt so ashamed. I knew it was irrational — I knew that this could happen to anyone and that there was nothing to be embarrassed about. But still, reasonable or not, I flushed with mortification.

The subway was dank with sour odors, and I needed to come up for oxygen.

Maybe if I go outside, I'll get revived by the fresh air and I'll be able to think more clearly. Or better yet, maybe I'll find the money I need obligingly dropped on the sidewalk right at the top of the subway steps!

These were the two better-case scenarios I concocted in my head, as I ascended the stairs. But what awaited me outside was better than anything I could possibly have conceived in my wildest imagination.

A yellow taxicab — one of the tens of thousands that rove Manhattan's streets — had just pulled up to the curb and was in the process of discharging a passenger.

My heart leaped when I spotted it, and without a moment's hesitation, I slid into the front seat as soon as the passenger stepped out.

"I can't believe this!" I exclaimed, dizzy with relief. "This is what you call perfect timing. How did you know to be at the corner of Broadway and Forty-second Street at precisely 5:02 P.M. just as I emerged from the station?"

"God must have sent me," my husband the cabdriver chuckled, as he turned on the "Off Duty" sign indicating the end of his 12-hour day.

"Home?" he asked.

"Home," I sighed contentedly.

"Always at your service," he said as he swept off his cap in a mocking motion.

"You or God?" I shot back in response.

— *Claire Halberstam*

ᘏᕉᕐ

Comment

When it comes to receiving a divine gift, the amount of money involved may be minimal, but the value of the gift is surely priceless.

Charlie Grant was just one of the many stroke patients at Chicago's Cook County Hospital tended to by an array of practitioners, one of whom was nurse's aide Titus Virgil. Titus wished she could be more attentive to each and every individual under her care, but harried and overworked, she had little personal time to spend with any of her charges, including Charlie. As she rushed about her chores—emptying bed pans, straightening sheets—she engaged in casual chit-chat, but conversation was limited and rarely meaningful. She knew little about her patients, and they, in turn, knew even less about her.

But one thing she did want them to know, including Charlie Grant, was her name, and he kept on forgetting it. One day, she showed him her hospital identification card to help him remember. As she pointed her name out to him and pronounced it in a loud and clear voice, she was oblivious to the visitor sitting at Charlie Grant's bedside.

"Titus," she articulated slowly. "T-i-t-u-s."

The visitor—who happened to be Charlie Grant's brother, Joseph—registered mild surprise at her unusual name.

"I had a daughter named Titus," he offered casually. "But that was so many years ago. . . ."

He didn't think of pursuing the conversation, but Titus on the other hand wouldn't consider dropping it.

"Did your daughter have a middle name?" she pressed.

"Yes," Joseph Grant answered, "a strange name that her mother had insisted upon—Sabato."

It was then that Titus began to cry and understanding first dawned upon Joseph.

"Oh my God," he screamed, "I've found my daughter!"

The two had been searching for each other for over forty years. By chance, they had ended up in the same Cook County Hospital room, caring for Charlie Grant.

"It was miraculous the way we met," said Titus, who hadn't seen her father since she was six years old.

Joseph Grant had separated from his wife in the 1950s, but remained in touch with his two daughters, Titus and Josephine, then six and seven. He visited them regularly and loved them with all his heart.

"But one week I came to their apartment and they had moved," he remembers sadly. No forwarding address had been left behind. Neighbors said they had no information. Joseph Grant's beloved children had vanished, and it was as if they had ceased to exist.

But not in his mind, not in his heart. He scoured the city streets for them, "driving up and down blocks in different Chicago neighborhoods, going to different schools to look for them." Decades later, he was still thumbing his way through Chicago's white pages phone book, dialing up dozens of women with the same name as his ex-wife. But unbeknownst to him, she had remarried and had a new surname. His efforts were in vain. "But still . . . I never gave up."

Titus's phone book was also well thumbed. She too had raked its pages for decades, seeking clues to her father's whereabouts. But for her as well, the phone book proved to be a dead end; it yielded no signs, no hints, no trails to her father's home or heart. Grant, after all, is a very common name, so common in fact, that when Charlie Grant became one of her patients, she didn't give his name a second thought.

"What's in a name?" Shakespeare asks in Romeo and Juliet. "That which we call a rose by any other name would smell just as sweet."

Shakespeare is wrong. Sometimes a name can change your destiny, shape your life, reunite you with a long-lost father.

What's in a name? Ask Titus Virgil. That's T-i-t-u-s.

*T**hree* generations of Sanchezes had yielded no male progeny, so when a baby boy was finally born to Alina, her grandparents rejoiced.

"There was nothing they wouldn't or couldn't do for Jimmy," Alina remembers fondly. "They basically lived for him. He was pampered, humored, indulged. They baby-sat him constantly and visited often. Their love for him was endless."

But when Jimmy was only two, his great-grandfather died, so it was with his great-grandmother Magda (whom he called Aba) that he forged his deepest bond.

Magda was old in years but young in spirit. She was a typical great-grandmother in that she was loving, kind, and warm and baked delicious homemade cookies. She was atypical in that it was she who taught Jimmy how to climb a fence, ride a bike, and slide a scooter across the street. Everyone marveled at their kinship and affinity. Even as Jimmy got older and his contemporaries began to lose interest in their grandparents, his profound love for his great-grandmother endured.

In 1994, when Jimmy was only 22, he was gunned down in a senseless street mugging. He was shot in the heart by a 19-year-old who wanted his watch.

Alina didn't know how to tell her grandmother that Jimmy was dead.

"I thought she would just crumble," Alina remembers, "but it was *she* who ended up supporting *me*, not the other way around. She was very present, very there for me. I couldn't have continued without her help."

Five years later, in 1999, Magda Sanchez died at the age of 95.

"She had a full life and of course we were very grateful for all the years we had together, but still, how could we not be sad? We had lost our dear Aba and we were in a lot of pain," says Alina.

The night before the funeral, family and friends gathered at the funeral parlor for the viewing. The chapel contained several different rooms, so when it was time to leave, Alina used the key that the chapel director had given her to lock the room that contained Magda's coffin.

It was then that she first noticed the guestbook near the door that visitors are asked to sign before entering a chapel to pay their respects.

"What should we do with the guestbook?" Alina's mother asked in a worried tone, following her gaze.

"Let's just leave it here and we'll take it home tomorrow, when the funeral is over, okay?" Alina responded.

"Are you sure it's all right?" her mother fretted. "Maybe we should take it home for the night."

"Don't worry, it'll be fine."

Her mother's concern prompted Alina to glance casually at the guestbook and scan the names that had been scribbled into its pages.

"I have never looked at a guestbook before," Alina says, "but something just made me take a look. I noticed that the very last signature in the book belonged to my engaged daughter's future mother-in-law, Rosalind Jorge. Then I turned off the lights, locked the door, and closed up for the night."

The next day, the family returned to the funeral home to gather for the procession to the church where the mass would take place. "I was the first to arrive at the funeral parlor," Alina recalls, "and the only one with the key to our room. As I entered, I noticed my mother's friend waiting outside for us to open the chapel door. I greeted her, unlocked the door, and headed straight for the guestbook."

In retrospect, Alina remains puzzled by her own action.

"I've never looked at guestbooks before," she insists again. "They never interested me in the slightest." But because her mother had seemed so anxious about the guestbook the night before, something drew her to the stand on which it was placed, to check to see that the pages were still intact.

It was then that she saw the entry.

JIMMY FENTON, with a little cross next to it (indicating deceased) was written in a childish scrawl, right below Rosalind Jorge's signature — the last name entered into the book before Alina had closed up the night before.

"The handwriting was not that of an adult," Alina says, "but clearly one belonging to a young child. It reminded me of the peculiar way Jimmy used to sign his name when he was in grade school."

Staring in disbelief at the signature in the book, Alina thought she would faint. Trembling, she turned toward the woman who had entered the chapel with her. "Was there anyone near or outside the chapel when you got here?" Alina demanded.

"No," the woman answered, puzzled by Alina's feverish state.

"Did you notice this signature in the book?" Alina asked, pointing to Jimmy's entry.

"Yes, I did," the woman said, "which is why I entered my name two lines underneath."

"And you didn't see anyone hanging around here earlier?" Alina pressed again.

"Absolutely not."

When Alina's daughter and husband arrived a few minutes later at the chapel, she pounced on them, frenzied, insisting they tell her if either one of them had entered Jimmy's name in the guestbook.

They looked at her in shock. "Why would we ever do a thing like that?" they asked.

No one could understand who or why someone would pull a prank like that. Or was it a prank?

When Alina returned from the cemetery that day with the guestbook in hand, she hunted for a scrapbook she had helped Magda compile during the last days of her life—a scrapbook that contained old photographs, tattered mementos, ancient letters, faded notes. And, Alina remembered, an old Valentine's Day card from Jimmy to his beloved Aba. He had given it to his great-grandmother when he was only eight years old.

When Alina found the little Valentine's Day card tucked into the scrapbook, she opened it and studied the handwriting. Then she spread open the guestbook to the page that contained Jimmy's entry.

The handwriting was exactly the same.

"Jimmy always had a very distinctive way of printing his name," Alina remembers. "It wasn't similar to other childish scrawls, but very idiosyncratic and unique. It wasn't a handwriting you would easily confuse with someone else's."

Studying the evidence before her very eyes, Alina could only come up with one conclusion: Jimmy had loved his great-grandmother so much that he had come to pay his respects at her funeral. And he loved his family so much that he had come to be with them to share their grief.

"We felt that we had been given a sign from above, a reassurance from Jimmy, that one day we would all be together," is the way Alina interprets the baffling event.

"The dead are here with us," she says, passionate and resolute. "They may not be here physically, but surely they're here in spirit."

❧

Comment
The line between this world and the next seems, at times, no sharper than that drawn by a fine-tipped pen.

*O*n May 2, 1997, four-year-old Joshua Kelton was diagnosed with aggressive leukemia.

For two weeks, he had been experiencing fluctuating night temperatures of 103 to 105 degrees, lack of appetite, and chronic fatigue. The first doctor his parents consulted in Honolulu noticed that Joshua's ears looked pink and prescribed amoxicillin. The second doctor they visited, one week later when the symptoms stubbornly remained, placed a ruler on the floor and asked Joshua to jump over it. He couldn't. Hiding his alarm, the doctor casually suggested that the Keltons see a friend of his at the Army Medical Center. It was only after Joshua's blood had been drawn and analyzed that the "friend" introduced himself.

"Let me explain who I am," the doctor said gently, after examining the blood results. "I'm a hematologist. The reason why Joshua is here today is because your son has leukemia."

The Keltons—Elizabeth and Herb—broke down.

Afterwards, Herb Kelton composed himself, looked the doctor squarely in the eye, and asked, "What do we have to do to help our son?"

Joshua's white blood cell count was well over the half-million mark and he was rushed to the intensive care unit to be stabilized. Then he endured a protocol of chemotherapy for three months, after which he was pronounced "in remission."

"But," cautioned the doctor, "this type of leukemia is aggressive. If Joshua relapses, it won't be that easy to bring him back to remission."

He relapsed only two weeks later.

Joshua went back on chemotherapy and remained on it for the next nine months, but doctors remained guarded. "If he relapses one more time," they warned, "the only course of treatment left will be a bone marrow transplant."

It was a harsh reality the Keltons had to face and prepare for. They had themselves and their daughter—Joshua's only sibling—tested to see if their bone marrow matched their son's, but the news was discouraging.

"We'll have to go to the National Bone Marrow Registry to see if we can find a match," the doctors said.

But because the Keltons are a mixed-race couple, finding bone marrow that matched six out of six markers was particularly challenging. No match could be found.

"What if we were to get pregnant?" Evelyn Kelton asked Joshua's doctor one day. "Is it conceivable that the baby's bone marrow could match Joshua's?"

Herb Kelton's jaw dropped as he heard his wife query the physician. They had decided a long time ago that they would not have any more children.

"Honey," he interjected gently, "I don't think we should consider having another baby at this time."

"Nonetheless," she pressed on, "I want to know . . . what are the chances that the baby could be a match?"

"Well," the doctor answered, "statistics say one in four. Those aren't such bad odds, you might think. On the other hand, you could have a hundred babies and none would end up being a match. And," he added, "even if the baby should be a match, there's no guarantee that we can keep Joshua in remission for nine months."

Evelyn was undeterred by the daunting odds.

Later, when they were alone, she repeated to Herb: "Honey, time is running out. We have to do something. Let's get pregnant!"

"But what if the baby got sick . . . just like Joshua?" Herb worried.

"We have to think positive!" Evelyn said stubbornly.

"But the doctor himself said there's only a 25 percent chance that the baby would be a match," Herb argued.

"We have to try!" Evelyn insisted.

"But Joshua's really sick. He might not be able to wait for a baby to be born. He might not make it another nine months . . . ," Herb continued to protest.

Evelyn's tone remained firm—firmer than he had ever heard it before. "We have to try."

It had taken six months to conceive Joshua, so the Keltons didn't have much hope of conceiving a baby immediately. The possibility was, in fact, so remote that when Evelyn felt ill two weeks later, she hastened to the emergency room of the local hospital, convinced she had a bad case of the flu.

"You're pregnant," the ER resident told her, after the blood tests came back.

It had taken six months to conceive Joshua. . . . How could she be pregnant so soon?

The pregnancy happened so easily and so quickly that deep inside her the conviction grew that this unborn child would prove to be Joshua's salvation.

"This baby is going to save Joshua's life!" Evelyn exclaimed.

When Evelyn was five months pregnant, doctors performed an amniocentesis procedure to determine whether the markers of the fetus corresponded with Joshua's.

"All six markers are exactly the same," doctors said when they got the test results. "The baby is a perfect match!"

Meanwhile, time was running out for Joshua.

"We can't wait until the baby is full-term," doctors tersely told the Keltons when Evelyn was in her seventh month of pregnancy. "We'll do a test to determine if the baby's lungs are strong enough, and if they are, we'll induce an early labor."

Later that day, Evelyn got the call. "Pack your bags," the hospital told her, "you're giving birth tomorrow."

On July 15, 1998, Justin Kelton was born, a surprisingly strapping six-pounder for an almost-two-months-premature baby. Since Justin wasn't old enough to donate his bone marrow, doctors removed stem cell blood from his umbilical cord instead, a procedure that had been successfully performed in the past. The blood was airlifted to a processing center in Utah and from there shipped to Stanford University Medical Center, where the actual transplant took place three weeks later.

Today, Joshua is a healthy, active seven year old, and Justin is a mischievous 20-month-old toddler.

"The two boys are real close . . . like twins," says Evelyn Kelton. "Every time Justin gets sick, Joshua gets sick too. They like the same clothes, same food, same toys . . . everything. They are connected in a very deep way. They are truly blood brothers . . . in every sense of the word."

As a female deputy sheriff working in Hillsborough County, Florida, I've certainly had my fair share of hair-raising experiences, but one particular episode that occurred six years ago unnerves me to this day.

In 1994, I was working the midnight shift and patrolling an area that was mostly rural. It had been a quiet night, unpunctuated by crises or diversions of any kind, and I was feeling kind of restless. At about two o'clock in the morning, however, I received a call from the police dispatcher. A van was stuck on the railroad tracks approximately seven miles away from my position.

I sped toward the site. Approaching the tracks in my car, I was alarmed to see a train, loaded with phosphates, racing toward the van. It was on an inevitable collision course with the van, and I was the only one who knew the fate that awaited both the oblivious train crew and the passengers inside the stranded vehicle. The enormity of this pressed upon me: Only I possessed this knowledge and only I had the ability to stop a terrible accident from occurring. The adrenaline coursed through my body.

I radioed my dispatcher and tersely reported that a train was headed toward the van. I knew that the engineer needed a mile's notice to slam down the brakes effectively, and I told the dispatcher to get in touch with him fast. The van was stalled on a curve of the train tracks, and unless he had prior warning, the engineer would never see it until it was too late.

I outraced the train and when I arrived at the scene, I saw an empty van sitting on the tracks, abandoned by its occupants. I was relieved that the van passengers were no longer in the path of danger, but the train crew still was. If the train hit the van, it would derail for sure. Serious injuries—or even death—could result from such a wreck.

I called my dispatcher again. She said she could not make contact with the train, but would keep on trying. My adrenaline pumped.

I tried to park my cruiser and run my emergency lights, but I was stymied. A swamp abutted one side of the tracks, and the other side was fenced in with cattle. I was forced to park almost 200 feet away and found myself in the yard of the only house in the area.

An elderly gentleman and his young grandson ran out of the house to meet me. It was from this house that the call to the police dispatcher had originally been made. The man had been the one who had sighted the van, and he had also seen an unruly group of teenagers leave the vehicle and flee on foot.

I called the dispatcher again. She still had not been able to establish contact with the crew. Far off in the distance, I could hear the rumble of the train. The quiet country night echoed its whistle.

I tried to push the van off the tracks, but it wouldn't budge an inch. The residents of the house could not be a source of assistance, either. The elderly man was too frail to help me, and his grandson was too young.

I picked up the phone to call the dispatcher again. This time I frantically shouted that it was an emergency! Equally frustrated, the dispatcher yelled back that she hadn't been able to reach the engineer but that she was trying hard.

I could feel the train's vibrations as I stood helpless on the tracks, panic-stricken. Which way do I run? I wondered. Who will find my body? I could see the train's light shining through the trees around the bend.

I felt powerless to halt the inevitable head-on collision. There was nothing left that I could do. I had no choice but to move the three of us—the elderly man, his grandson, and myself—to higher ground and safety. His house adjoined the railroad tracks, and if the crash happened, the train cars might crumple up accordion style in his yard and maybe even smash into his house.

"Is there anyone else in the house?" I yelled.

"My wife, she's sleeping. . . ."

"Wake her up fast, and get into my car." I would attempt to race away from the crash site as fast as I could.

It was then, in the early morning darkness, down a dirt frontage road, that a teenage boy in a pickup truck suddenly appeared. Blond, wearing a baseball cap and chewing tobacco, he pulled up alongside me and asked in an easygoing manner, "You need some help, officer?"

"I've got to get that van off the tracks before the train hits it!"

"I've got a tow rope; I'll have it off in a jiffy," he replied calmly, and then gunned his motor as he raced toward the tracks. Apprehensive, I followed on foot and returned to the site I had just evacuated. I knew that we would both be in mortal danger if he couldn't remove the van fast enough, but I couldn't let him go alone.

Within a matter of 30 seconds he had the van off the tracks, and the whole scenario changed. The collision would be avoided. The train crew would be saved. They would never even know how close to derailment—and death—they had come.

Elated and exhausted at the same time, I made my way back to reassure the elderly man and his grandson, who were still standing in the front yard some 25 feet away. "The van is off the tracks!" I shouted, dizzy with relief.

"And here comes the train now!" the man pointed.

Trembling, we watched as it peacefully whizzed by. We shook our heads in disbelief, shock, and awe. We were overcome by thoughts of the near calamity that had been averted at, literally, the last possible moment.

I turned to the elderly man and his grandson and took their names and other pertinent information for my official police report. Then I thought about the teenage boy, who surely deserved a police commendation for his heroism.

"Now if you'll excuse me," I apologized to the two, "I need to go talk to the boy in the truck who pulled the van off the tracks."

The elderly man looked confused. "What boy?" he asked.

I gestured toward the van that had been towed to the dirt road alongside the railroad tracks. "You know, the young man who used his truck to move the van," I happily reminded him.

"No disrespect, ma'am, but nobody's been down this road but you."

I hurried down to the train tracks and to the van that sat beside it.

The boy, his tow rope, and his truck were gone.

The van remained on the side of the tracks; it had clearly been pulled off. But to this day I do not know who hauled it out of danger's reach that fateful night.

—*Jennifer Greco*

❧

Comment

Some miracles illuminate the world, and others remain forever hidden in the darkness of night.

*M*y father was ill in Denver; I lived in New York, where family obligations and small children kept me home, waiting for news. He had cancer and it was terminal; but the doctor could offer no prognosis. *It could be months or it could be days,* he said.

One night, a dream transported me back to my childhood home in Pittsburgh, where my father had lived the bulk of his life. In the dream, I clearly saw the winding staircase that led from the second floor to the third, and on the flight of stairs my father stood, bathed in an aura of light. The light was unlike anything I had ever seen in this earthly world; it was dazzling, resplendent, and very strong.

My father's back was turned to me as he ascended the staircase slowly. I felt a tremendous sense of loss as I saw him mount the steps; the sensation was poignant and knifed my heart. I wanted to call out to him, but something held me back; I was struck mute. Then suddenly, he turned around, looked directly at me standing at the bottom of the landing, smiled tenderly, and raised his arm in greeting. But it was not hello that he waved with his hand; it was clearly good-bye.

Just then the phone rang and woke me from my dream. It was my sister in Denver informing me that our father had just passed away. She was surprised at my calm response.

I was calm because I felt certain that my father had appeared in my dream to bid me a final farewell. I was calm because I was confident that his spirit would continue to watch over me, long after his body had turned to dust. And I felt calm because I knew, beyond a shadow of a doubt, that he was surely in paradisiacal realms. For I had seen him on the stairway, making his gradual ascent toward heaven.

—*Claire Halberstam*

Comment
The pain of passage can be eased greatly by a simple gesture of love.

In 1992, my daughter Sinaya was treated for a certain medical condition and, as part of her treatment, was given a very potent drug. It was only a few weeks later that she learned something that would become for her— simultaneously—both cause for joy and a source of unremitting horror.

She discovered that she had been pregnant when she had ingested the medication and that the powerful drug was one that was known to cause birth defects.

She and her husband agonized over what to do. This was their first child. They had originally greeted the news of the pregnancy with great elation. But now they were seized with dread and panic at the possible consequences of the medication. To bring a deformed baby into this world! It was too cruel.

Their doctor had not been able to give them the assurances they wanted to hear. *It was very possible*, he had said, *that the baby would be born perfectly normal. Then again*, he had said, *it was possible that the baby might not be normal at all.*

After many nights of soul-searching, the couple made their decision. They would not abort, but would proceed with the pregnancy.

Still, Sinaya couldn't stop herself from worrying throughout the pregnancy. Given the reality of the situation, her obsession was understandable. She was constantly besieged with nightmare visions of a grossly deformed baby cradled in her arms. As the pregnancy progressed, she became increasingly tense and anxious. My heart ached for my daughter. Her pain was too much to bear. I couldn't take it anymore; I felt I had to do something concrete to obliterate—or at least diminish— her torment.

For many years, I had been told amazing stories about a contemporary Jewish sage/saint known as the Lubavitcher Rebbe. He was an internationally famous Hasidic rabbi who, people said, performed miracles. Although I was not a constituent of his group, nor did I know anyone within his fold, I decided to reach out to him for help.

I faxed a letter to his office, asking for a blessing for my daughter's unborn child. The very next day, I received a phone call from a man who identified himself as Rabbi Groner, the Rebbe's personal secretary. He had a message for me from the Rebbe, he said. The baby was going to be perfectly healthy, normal, and well, and he would grow up to be a fine and wonderful human being. I was delirious with joy, dizzy with relief. "Rabbi Groner," I asked, "do you promise this is true?"

"The Rebbe promises that everything will be fine. *Mazel tov* (Congratulations)."

That night, Sinaya called me to report that her water had just broken and that she was on her way to the hospital.

"Sinaya," I told her, "don't be afraid of anything. You got a blessing from the Rebbe today and he promised that everything will be okay."

As I hung up, I glanced at the clock, saw that it was 8 P.M., and was startled to realize an uncanny coincidence. Exactly 25 years before, on the exact same date, also at 8 P.M. in the evening, my own water had broken—and later that night, I had given birth to Sinaya!

Sinaya gave birth the next morning to a robust, sturdy, healthy baby boy whom she named Ariel. We were vastly relieved and exceedingly grateful to hear the doctors declare him perfectly normal in every way. I also felt indebted to the Lubavitcher Rebbe, whose blessing, I felt sure, had served as a protective shield and had been instrumental in assuring my grandson's uneventful delivery and safe birth.

Five years later, I was in my home in Miami when my phone began to ring insistently. Sinaya's voice—garbled, hysterical, frenzied—came on the line, shrieking that she had accidentally slammed down the door of the car trunk on Ariel's head and that he was critically hurt. She screamed for me to rush to Memorial Hospital, fast.

As my son drove me from North Miami Beach to Hollywood, Florida, I shuddered at the injuries I imagined Ariel had sustained. As our car turned onto the highway, a large white van pulled in front of us and continued ahead of us at a steady clip. Suddenly I began to scream. Emblazoned on the back of the van was an oversized portrait of . . . the Lubavitcher Rebbe! I could not believe my eyes. I grabbed my son's shoulder and pointed to the picture. Seeing the Rebbe's face on the back of that van totally unhinged me. I began to scream at the picture that loomed before me, as if I were addressing an actual person.

"You promised!" I shrieked. "You *promised*. You said he would grow up healthy and well. Help him! Help me!"

Still, in spite of my suffering, I couldn't help but be struck by the wonder of it all: the strangeness of that van's presence in our lane. All the way to the hospital, the van never changed its course or moved from its position. It remained right in front of us the whole time, never once veering from our path. It almost seemed as if the van were escorting us straight to the hospital door. As soon as we arrived at the emergency room entrance, it vanished from sight.

Inside the reception area, my daughter was waiting in a pool of red, her arms wrapped around Ariel. Pale and frightened, the child was a terrifying specter, hemorrhaging from his head and drenched in blood. When Sinaya saw us, an animal-like howl of pure anguish tore from her lips. Without a word, she thrust Ariel into my arms and ran screaming out the door.

Ariel was bleeding profusely, and soon another pool of blood collected under my own feet. I didn't think he would survive.

But when the doctor saw Ariel, he assured us that his condition looked far worse than it actually was. The blood pouring out of his head was coming from one ruptured vein, and the doctor quickly stitched up the wound. When I told the doctor that a trunk door had been slammed down hard on Ariel's head, he marveled that the child had escaped with such minor injuries, considering the severity of the blow.

"It's a miracle," I said.

One year later, I impulsively decided to attend prayer services at an unfamiliar synagogue in Miami Beach, where I am not a member and where I have no acquaintances. After services, the worshipers were invited to a lavish spread of pastries and wine, and it was there that I first noticed a little elderly man with sidelocks and beard. I have always been attracted to otherworldly types, so I made a beeline to him and boldly introduced myself. He told me that his name was Rabbi Dolphin and that he was a disciple of the Lubavitcher Rebbe. I was excited to share my personal encounter with the Rebbe's miraculous healing powers and told him the story of the blessing, the accident, and the mysterious van.

When I finished my story, his eyes twinkled and he said, "Would you like to meet the lady who was driving the van that day?" He motioned to his side a woman whom he introduced as Miriam.

Miriam, he told me, had dedicated her life to spreading the teachings of the Lubavitcher Rebbe, and toward that end, had purchased a van in which religious paraphernalia was stored. She had a "billboard" of the Rebbe on the back of her vehicle, so that his luminous visage would bless motorists and pedestrians alike. How far that blessing extended, Miriam could never have known.

—*Devorah Alouf*

❧

Comment
Within the blessing of a holy being lies the power to protect us from mortal danger and restore us to spiritual health.

*M*y brother's life had been ravaged by drugs.

We had tried to help him, support him, get him off the drugs. He had served a prison term of three years, and when he was finally discharged, we thought for sure that he'd come to his senses and would start life anew.

Behind bars, James was a model prisoner. He had been rehabilitated and had forsworn the ruinous path he had previously walked. To everyone within earshot, he declared loud and clear that when he reentered "civilian life" he would never go near drugs again. He was so unwavering and fierce in his determination to cast away his previous existence that he became a veritable force within the prison system itself. He discovered that he had a talent for oratory, and he became a motivational speaker. The prison took him to local schools, where he lectured teenagers on the perils of drug addiction. In the penitentiary, James was an absolute star.

But once he got out, something broke inside of him. Within a few short months of his release from prison, the vicious circle had begun again. Many people suspected the truth early on, but I remained clueless. Perhaps it was because he was my little brother whom I loved so much. Or maybe it was because I simply couldn't read what were, for others, telltale signs. But I, for one, did not know that James was back on drugs and in an inevitable spiral of destruction.

One day James came to the apartment where I lived, with his pregnant wife and two small children in tow. He was utterly broke and asked if I could lend him $10 so that he could buy his kids milk and diapers. Because I had no cash on me, I gave him a check for the amount he requested. He thanked me profusely.

In fact, his thanks were too profuse. They were excessive, extravagant, and certainly not commensurate with the amount I had lent him. He thanked me endlessly and kept emphasizing over and over again: "Don't worry, Pat—no matter what, I will get you the $10 back."

He didn't say it once; he didn't say it twice; he didn't say it three times. He must have reiterated the same sentence at least 20 times.

Finally, I found myself getting irritated by his behavior. This was not characteristic; it wasn't like him to repeat himself in this way. "All right, enough already!" I shouted. "How many times are you going to say the same thing?"

But even in the driveway, as he left with my check, he turned around to repeat three more times: "I promise you'll get it back."

Only seven days later, James overdosed on drugs, and he was gone—my only sibling. I went to the local florist shop and sadly ordered flowers for his funeral. I couldn't believe that James, my beloved brother, was dead.

I was in such a state of shock, in fact, that I forgot my checkbook at home and didn't have the money to pay for the order. Embarrassed, I assured the store owner that I would return in a few days, when I was more composed, to pay my bill.

The following week, before heading to town, I hunted for the checkbook so that I could fulfill my promise to the florist. As I put the checkbook in my bag, I mused that the very last time I had used it was when I had written the $10 loan for James. Now, only two weeks later, I was again using it to cover his expenses—but this time, it was for flowers for his funeral.

It gave me a chill.

As I advanced toward the door of the florist shop, something fluttered on the sidewalk in front of me.

A brand-new, crisp $10 bill, looking as though it had been freshly minted, fluttered on the concrete. It looked so spanking-clean, so untouched-by-human-hands new, in fact, that I was sure it was either a fake or a joke.

As I bent down to retrieve it, I searched the street for a torn envelope flapping somewhere nearby or an anxious face peering for a lost bill. I could find neither.

But as I picked it up, I knew in my heart that no one would ever come to claim the bill, for the $10 was clearly meant for me.

James had kept his last promise.

My brother may have had a lot of personal problems, but he was always true to his word.

—*Pat Malone*

❦

Comment
Integrity, like love, transcends worlds.

*C*hris and Joe began dating in high school in 1985, when they were 15 and 16 years old, respectively. It was the first serious relationship for both, and Chris was sure that what she was experiencing was positively, absolutely "true love." The two dated each other exclusively for four years—until they were both in college—and then Chris's world caved in.

One day, in 1989, Joe told Chris that while he cared deeply about her, he wanted to play the field a little . . . test the waters. "You know, we were quite young when we started dating and the only one I've ever really been involved with has been you," he said. "I think it would be smart for us to see other people. For me, marriage is a lifelong commitment, and we should make sure we're right for one another. We need a basis for comparison."

For the first time in her life, Chris grasped the meaning of that well-worn phrase "a broken heart."

"My heart ached for him last thing at night before I fell asleep and ached for him first thing in the morning when I woke up," she vividly remembers.

Still, she would not deny him his wish. "Deep in my heart I felt certain that he was the one—the only one—for me and that I truly loved him, but I went along with his plan, despite my own misgivings. I never breathed a word of protest or opposition. After all, he was the one who had initiated the breakup, and I was too proud to try to reestablish ties."

A year and a half passed. Occasionally, the two would telephone each other just to "check in," but during this entire period, they remained firm about adhering to the provisions of the breakup. Despite the fact that they both lived in a relatively small area in Maine, they never encountered one another anywhere, not even once.

In September 1990, Chris was dating a nice guy named Mike, who was known for his spontaneity and joie de vivre.

One evening, he impulsively asked Chris: "Hey, how about driving to Boston and seeing if we can get standby tickets for tonight's Red Sox game?"

Even though they were about an hour away from Boston, Chris didn't mind acting on a whim. "I heard tonight's game is sold out," she said, "but we certainly can try. Maybe we'll get lucky!"

At Boston's Fenway Park, they discovered to their chagrin that the game was indeed sold out, but they decided to wait around anyway. The reward for their exemplary patience was two prized tickets for admission to—yes!—that night's game.

As she settled into her seat, Chris found herself facing the walkway, and it was there that she suddenly glimpsed a flash of familiar red hair. She gulped and thought: Oh, no, it can't be!

But it was.

Her beloved Joe, whom she hadn't seen for 18 months, was coming down the walkway with his current flame, Diane. All over the small Maine town she lived in, the grapevine had buzzed that the two were a serious "item." Chris couldn't bear seeing the pair together. It was one thing to hear about Joe's active social life and quite another to have to witness it herself. So she looked away and soothed herself silently: *Don't say anything, don't greet him, it's okay, he'll probably just walk straight on by and never even notice you. . . .*

Just then, people in her row began standing up to let a couple squeeze past to get to their seats.

Joe inspected the numbers on his tickets, glanced at the seats, saw Chris sitting next to one of them, and their eyes locked. Joe examined his ticket once again, and, jaw dropping in disbelief, reluctantly slid into his seat . . . right next to Chris.

"Well, this is kinda interesting . . . ," Chris murmured softly to the shaken man beside her.

But Joe stared straight ahead, unblinking. In an obvious gesture, he opened his program wide, scrutinized it with intense interest, and kept his eyes determinedly on the field without diverting his gaze once. During the entire game, he was uncharacteristically quiet. He didn't talk to his date, Diane, nor did he utter a single word to Chris. He was, in fact, speechless.

Chris could have felt rebuffed and hurt, but instead, she returned home strangely elated.

"Thirty-five thousand seats at Fenway Park, and he gets to sit right next to me!" she thought. "This has to be a sign."

Meanwhile, elsewhere in a small town in Maine, Joe's date, Diane, was recapitulating the exact same scene in her mind.

"I knew right then," she told Joe, "we were done."

The next day, an emboldened Chris called Joe and said, "How weird was that?"

They began comparing notes about what they had both been thinking and feeling at the stadium, and they laughed about the coincidence.

Eleven months later, they were married, and their 10th anniversary is coming up soon.

❧

Comment
God employs a large squadron of helpers, some of whom do nothing more outstanding than sell tickets at the local sports arena.

*J*ody Robbins* didn't believe in the prophetic power of dreams, but this particular one had been vivid and disturbing.

She shivered when the dream roused her from her sleep in the middle of the night. She had seen her elderly mother's home engulfed in flames, and, in the dream, her mother was burned beyond recognition.

The clock at her bedside announced that it was three in the morning, and as much as Jody wanted to call her mother at that very moment and be reassured by the sound of her comforting voice, she also didn't want to stress her already fragile heart. So Jody promised herself that she would call her mother first thing in the morning and tell her about the ominous dream.

But when she called, her mother—independent, self-sufficient, and a skeptic to boot—only laughed. She was more psychologically than psychically oriented, and she scolded Jody in a bantering voice: "So is this then your secret wish . . . that I die?"

Jody wasn't offended; she knew it was her mother's feeble attempt to disarm her, to diminish her concern. But she couldn't be swayed from her conviction that the dream had been portentous; it was too powerful to shrug off so lightly.

"Mom!" she began to plead in protest, when suddenly she heard a familiar click on the line.

"Oh, there goes that darned call waiting again," her mother sighed. "Am I ever sorry that I signed up for that service from the phone company! All my calls keep getting interrupted, and I always end up insulting somebody. Hold on a minute, dear, while I take that call, and I'll be right back."

Her mother hated keeping people waiting, so Jody was surprised when several minutes elapsed and her mother still had not returned to her call.

That's strange, she thought. *Mom never keeps me waiting so long.* She was about to hang up when her mother's voice—now breathless—came back on the line.

"Oh, Jody," she apologized. "I'm so sorry. That was your sister Carol, calling from Hawaii, where you know she's been vacationing. . . ."

"Mom, didn't you tell me that Carol called you yesterday? Is everything okay with her? I mean, it's not like her to make so many long-distance calls!"

"Well, Jody, actually, Carol's call unnerved me just a little. . . . It's so strange," her mother laughed nervously, "but it seems that last night, Carol had the exact same dream you had."

"Mom!" Jody shrieked. "What did she dream exactly?"

"Jody, it's no use going over it. . . . Your dreams weren't similar. They were *identical.*"

"Well, then, Mom, that does it. No ifs, buts, or maybes. I want you to move in with me for a few days, and we'll get some professionals to inspect your house to make sure there are no fire traps or anything to beware of."

"Jody!" her mother said sharply. "That's ridiculous; you know I need my space and . . . I don't believe in dreams."

"Even when two sisters—halfway across the world from each other—have the exact same dream on the exact same night? It gives me goose bumps, Mom. If you don't want to do it for yourself, please do it for me."

The following night, a gas explosion erupted in Jody's mother's house, incinerating the house in a matter of minutes.

The house was destroyed, but Jody's mother was out of harm's way, thanks to her daughters' twin dreams. Over her loud, strenuous objections, Jody had driven a small van to her mother's house, packed two suitcases with clothes and her mother's most precious possessions, and said firmly, "You're staying with me."

So at the time of the fire, she was safely ensconced in her daughter's home.

ی‌ی‌ی‌

Comment

Since we don't always respond to a single note, the Universe occasionally turns up the volume and send its message in stereo.

*L*isa, my six-year-old daughter, was running a high temperature and had a mysterious infection on her leg.

"Have you ever heard of osteomyelitis?" asked our pediatrician gently, when he made the initial diagnosis. This rare bone disease had stricken my precious child. She had to be taken to UCLA Hospital, where she would be put on IV medication and observed. If this course of treatment failed, amputation might have to be considered as the next possible option.

It was 1968, and the ward was filled with children suffering from bone cancer. I felt so sad for them. Some were terminal cases. These children would never come home. In contrast, I knew with certainty that I would be bringing Lisa home, either with two legs or one. And for that, I was grateful.

Several days later her infection receded, and we were enormously thankful that Lisa would be coming home with two legs after all and much to talk about with her younger sister Terri.

In her own way four-year-old Terri had also been a casualty of this medical crisis. Even though I left her under the care of my devoted mother-in-law during the day, Terri still felt abandoned. I would depart for the hospital early every morning and not return until late in the evening to pick her up. The prolonged absence of both her parents and her older sister was a genuine trauma for Terri. When I put her to bed each night after prayers and a story, she would cry for her sister. "Where's Lisa?" she would sob. "Why isn't she here with me?" I promised her that Lisa would be returning home from the hospital shortly and that soon they'd be sharing their bedroom and stories once again.

When the big day came, I was one anxious mom. Despite the fact that she was being discharged from the hospital, Lisa was still forbidden to walk for several more days, and the orthopedic physician warned me to be vigilant about keeping her off her feet. Hard to tell an active six-year-old child, harder yet to enforce!

When Terri and Lisa saw one another, they hugged and kissed, elated to be together again. But during naptime, I decreed, they would have to be apart to ensure that they slept. I sent Terri to the bedroom and put Lisa on the couch in the living room where I could keep her under close watch.

All this time my friend Carole had been keeping me company, and once both girls were safely tucked in, she suggested we take a break over a cup of coffee. I never drink coffee in the afternoon, but my nerves were frayed. Some peace and quiet and a chat with a dear friend, while companionably sipping coffee, seemed inviting. Carole headed to the kitchen to prepare a potful. I welcomed the thought of relaxing a little, for the first time in weeks.

The quiet that had momentarily fallen over the house was suddenly pierced by Terri's wails. She was sobbing in the bedroom. "I want Lisa to sleep here," she cried. "With me. You promised, Mommy. Why does she have to nap on the couch? You said she'd come back to our room as soon as she gets back from the hospital. I want Lisa!"

She wouldn't let up. Terri continued to weep, whimper, and whine, until I felt I would snap. I had really been tested the last couple of weeks and now that the crisis was over, my adrenaline had stopped pumping and exhaustion engulfed me instead. *A vacation on a small island would be nice,* I thought wearily. Having reached my breaking point, I was ready to do anything to get Terri to quit crying and take her nap, so I decided to move Lisa from the couch and let the girls be together in their room.

I had just put Lisa on her bed when I heard a thunderous noise.

My heart raced as I thought: *It's the big one. This was it,* I thought—*the major California earthquake we had been bracing ourselves for all our lives.* I ran into the kitchen to get Carole, and we both looked into the living room at the exact same time.

And there, in the middle of my living room, sat a very large Ford Fairlane car!

Carole and I stood speechless.

A woman and three small children were inside the car, shaken and crying. The woman explained that she had been driving down our street when she had lost control of the car and it had headed straight for the wall of my house. It had penetrated the wall and crashed straight into my living room.

After I helped the woman and her children climb out of the car and made sure that they were not injured, I looked around the living room to assess the damage. It was a complete disaster. But what really made me tremble was the sight of the couch that Lisa had been lying on only seconds before.

The couch looked like an accordion.

Had Terri not fussed about her sister's absence from their room, I never would have moved Lisa off that couch. And if I hadn't agreed—uncharacteristically—to an afternoon cup of coffee, Carole and I would still have been sitting in the living room when the accident occurred. All three of us—Lisa, Carole, and I—might very well have been killed.

I was still shaking when I called my husband at work. He couldn't believe my story. "Thank goodness, those Ford Fairlanes are really sturdy!" he said.

—*Colleen Ann Traphagen*

Comment

Like pieces in a chess game, we are constantly being guided to move here and there, out of harm's way, into a safe and protected space.

*W*hen I was in the eighth grade in Ohio, a girl who rode the same school bus that I did had a terrible accident. As she was racing to the bus so as not to miss it, she slipped on ice and fell under the rear wheels of the bus. She survived the accident but was paralyzed from the waist down.

I went to see her, and in my 13-year-old mind I thought that she wouldn't have much of a life now. Over the years, I moved, married, and had children, and didn't think much about Helen after that.

Three years ago, in Florida, my oldest son was hit by a car while riding his bike. He was thrown 90 feet and landed on his head, suffering a horrible brain injury. While semicomatose, he was transferred to a rehabilitation center.

I was in my son's room when the phone rang. It was a lady who said that she was the rehab's social worker. It was a particularly trying day. I burst into tears for no reason and heard the click of the call being disconnected.

A short time later, a beautiful woman in a wheelchair rolled into my son's room with a box of tissues. After 16 years, I still recognized Helen.

She smiled, handed me the tissues, and motioned for me to come closer. I did, and she hugged me. I told her who I was, and after we both got over the shock of finding each other after 16 years, she told me about her life since we had last seen each other. She was happily married, had children, and had gotten her degree so that she could smooth the path for those less fortunate than herself. She told me that if there was anything she could give me, it would be hope.

Looking at this wonderful, giving person, I felt small. But I also felt the hope she gave me, the first I had since learning that my son had been hurt. From this person whom I thought would have no quality of life, I learned never to give up—ever. And I learned that where there is life, there is hope.

My son miraculously recovered and we moved back north, but I owe Helen a debt that I can never adequately repay.

—Julie B. Gibson

❦

Comment
Within our own suffering can grow the compassion and wisdom to ease the suffering of others.

*M*y beloved husband, like others of his species (gender isn't strong enough a word to underscore the stark differences that exist between male and female!), takes personal pride in "beating traffic." There is no place for random impulses or spontaneous actions in attempting this Herculean feat. Unlike other well-known male habits (such as frenetic surfing of TV channels on the remote, never lingering long enough on one station to even catch a commercial), beating traffic is an exact science, requiring myriad maps of local roads and now-dusty highways, intense concentration, and savvy understanding of the human race. "Beating traffic" is a challenge that makes men's hearts race and women's shudder, a warrior's journey that far surpasses that second famous male test of mettle and endurance, otherwise known as "beating the light."

We were winding down after a long holiday weekend in upstate New York, and my husband had spent countless time considering the best way to "beat the traffic" home to Brooklyn. The final determination was that leaving in the middle of the night (1 A.M.) would achieve that lofty goal. Thus, it was about four in the morning (sigh!) when we finally reached our destination—home sweet home—and thoughts of finally tumbling into bed became less abstract and more real.

Trudging up the stairs behind my triumphant male (yes! he had beaten traffic! no one else was on the road . . .), my thoughts were on the soft pillows on which my head would soon be alighting, the downy quilts under which I would snuggle in cozy comfort.

Alas, it was not meant to be. My husband pulled out his keychain, and then in a dramatic motion more characteristic of *me* than *him*, smacked his forehead in rueful recollection and yelped: "Oh, my goodness, I left the house keys on the dining room table!"

Three sets of eyes (my own and those belonging to my two sons) gazed at him mournfully. Then he looked at me and said: "Well, what about *yours*?" Now, three sets of eyes were fixed on *me* with trust and hope.

In a small voice, I confessed: "I switched to my white pocketbook (after all, it's Memorial Day, it's fashionably correct now . . .) from my black pocketbook. And I (gulp . . . a little defensive) left the keys in the black pocketbook, sure that you had *yours* (good, back to offensive position!). . . ."

My in-laws and my mother had copies of our keys in their respective homes, but it was four o'clock in the morning, and we didn't want to wake them. They are over 70, and it wasn't fair to give them a jolt in the night.

"Okay," my husband said cheerfully, "we've never alarmed the house. I'm sure it's penetrable. I'll go around to the backyard and try to jimmy open the windows."

The good news was that the house is not penetrable. The bad news was that the house was not penetrable when we most desperately wanted it to be.

"Now what do we do?" We slumped on the stairs of our three-family dwelling. We were exhausted, bedraggled, and too tired to move. We had been up since seven o'clock the previous morning, almost 24 hours ago. We couldn't think straight.

"What we need right now is a small miracle!" my husband feebly quipped, semi-skeptic that he is.

Just then, as if on cue, the front door downstairs opened and in trooped our upstairs tenants, a young couple with a baby. They gazed at us in astonishment, and we returned the favor rather impolitely, as our mouths practically gaped open in disbelief.

"What are YOU doing here?" I asked in shock. "Aren't you supposed to be vacationing in New Jersey until tomorrow afternoon?"

"Yeah, well . . . ," the wife shrugged sheepishly. "We were supposed to stay until tomorrow but . . . my husband wanted to beat the traffic!"

Then she became aware of both our luggage and ourselves sprawled unseemingly across the hallway stairs. "And what about you?" she asked. "What are you doing here so early, and why aren't you inside your apartment?"

"We're locked out . . . ," I moaned. "The keys are on the dining room table. Big problem."

"You don't have a problem at all," she said. "Don't you remember that when I first moved in you gave me your keys? You said that if I ever needed anything, and you weren't home, just to use the keys and help myself?"

I didn't remember. But thankfully, she did.

"Yeah . . . sure I have your keys," she said happily. "And I know exactly where they are. Let me go get them."

As I fell into bed a few minutes later, I said to my husband: "See? You asked for a small miracle and that's precisely what you got!"

"It's a coincidence," he replied.

— *Yitta Halberstam*

❧

Comment

When you're half asleep, a small miracle can look just like a dull coincidence.

*H*e was as tall as I was short, as black as I was white, as Catholic as I was Jewish, as calm as I was excitable, as southern as I was Yankee. And for two decades, Bart Rousseve and I had been best friends.

During that time he'd been an usher at my wedding, godfather to my child, adviser through several job changes, confidant to my aspirations, confessor to my sins. I had nurtured him through his painful divorce and his brother's untimely death, cooked him gumbo when he was homesick, helped him decorate his apartment, and even chosen his eyeglass frames for him.

He was older and wiser. I was younger and warmer. We complemented each other perfectly, but the bond that kept us as close as the pages of a book was a shared faith in God.

We had two rituals. Every January, Bart would travel to South Africa as part of his job battling apartheid, and I would insist that he send me a postcard with a code message on it, indicating that he'd come to no harm. And every March, we would go out to dinner alone on a date halfway between our birthdays, which were just two weeks apart.

My husband thought my dependence on Bart was hilarious. "You won't be in touch with him for weeks on end, and then you'll insist on having him over five nights straight just before he leaves for Africa," he'd say.

"You don't understand," I'd reply; "it's not so much that I need to be with him, as that I need to know he's *there*."

Now, as I sat across from my beloved friend at our annual dinner just before his 53rd birthday in 1994, my worst fear came up and bit me.

"Molly, I have something to tell you," Bart said, reaching across the table and grabbing my hand. "I'm going to enter a monastery. It's too late for me to return to the priesthood, but I've given away my apartment and all my worldly goods, and I'm going to become a Franciscan friar."

Bart had been a Jesuit seminarian, but had reluctantly left just before taking his final vows because he did not believe himself capable of keeping a lifelong vow of celibacy. Although it was the swinging '60s, Bart would have been incapable of dishonoring his vows — that was not his way. But all his life, he'd felt he'd missed his calling, and now that he was older, he was confident of being able to keep all his vows. I felt selfish for regretting his news, but how in the world could I do without Bart?

"I know this is the right decision for you," I told him, "and for the greater good of the community. But darn it, what about *me*? How can you go off to a place where I can't call you every time I have a problem? What will I do without my best friend?"

"You can write me," he said gently. "I'm allowed to correspond with people. Our friendship won't end. It will just be a new dimension in the way we communicate."

"Oh, sure," I said bravely. But that night, I went home and wept. Of course, I tried to see Bart as often as possible over the ensuing months, but he was very busy as a United Nations observer to the first free elections in South Africa, and he had many other friends who also wanted his company. It was summer before we got to spend time alone again. He was to leave for the monastery in mid-August. One week earlier, we met for dinner. By coincidence, my husband was out of town on business. After my daughter—his goddaughter—went to bed, we sat on the couch, talking theology. At one point, we were discussing our different religions' views on the afterlife, and he leaned over and said, "You and I know there is no such thing as death, Molly. It's just a bridge to the next step of the journey."

As he left, I hugged him for long minutes, fighting back tears. "I'll miss you," I whispered. "Don't worry," he told me, *I'll still be here.*

Those words were etched into every thread of my being as, two weeks later, I got a phone call informing me that Bart had died in an automobile accident on August 14. "Nobody knows what happened," his sister Katherine told me. "He was driving up to the monastery, it was a sunny day, and there was no other traffic, but his car veered off the road and hit a tree, and he died instantly. We think he may have had a heart attack."

At the funeral, the priest who gave the eulogy said Bart had merely "skipped a step and gone straight to Saint Francis." But that was cold comfort to me. "Bart's dead," I sobbed on my husband's shoulder. "Never," he said firmly. "He is still alive in you."

"I know he's out there somewhere, but I just can't bear to let him go," I confided in Norbu Tsering, a friend from Tibet.

"In Buddhism," Norbu told me, "we believe that the soul remains in transition 49 days after death and is reborn on the seventh day of the seventh week. Since your friend led such an exemplary life, he is sure to have a fine reincarnation. Let yourself mourn him for seven weeks, and then celebrate on the 49th day.

I went home and checked the calendar. Bart's supposed "rebirthday" fell on October 2. That's my daughter's birthday.

I took solace from that and tried to be brave. But as October approached and I faced the first family birthday in 20 years without Bart, I became increasingly morose. The night before his "rebirthday," I slept fitfully, and I awoke the morning of October 2 in a foul mood. By what I viewed as a sadistic coincidence, my husband and I had to take our six-year-old downtown to someone else's birthday party that morning.

We hailed a taxi and tried to get onto the West Side Highway. But it was blocked by a funeral procession. "Can you believe this?" I raged to my husband. "When's the last time you saw a funeral procession on a highway? This is like some kind of sick cosmic joke."

It was an unseasonably warm and sunny day, and after the party, my husband suggested that we walk around the unfamiliar neighborhood to give me a chance to calm down. Soon we came upon El Teddy's, an offbeat restaurant I had always wanted to try. We tried to go in and grab a bite, but the staff met us at the door and told us the place was closed while they cleaned up from a private party. Then, spotting our little girl, one of the waiters said, "Oh, wait a minute! I have something to give you!" He ran inside and came out with a huge bunch of multicolored helium balloons with a single silver Mylar globe in the middle that said, "Happy Birthday."

That was it for me. My chest heaved. Tears rolled down my cheeks. "Thank you very much," my husband said quickly and, grabbing the balloons, rushed me over to a nearby park bench. "I've got an idea," he said brightly. "Let's send these balloons up to heaven to wish Bart a happy birthday."

"Oh, yes!" our daughter said, enchanted. "But can I keep one to take home?"

We assented, and after extricating the Mylar balloon from the middle, we released the bunch. "Happy birthday, dear Bart," we sang as the balloons soared into the robin's–egg blue sky and disappeared into cumulus clouds, "Happy birthday to you!"

When we got home, we let the Mylar balloon float to the middle of the living room ceiling, where it remained for a week. Then the helium started to leak out of it. But instead of falling to the floor, as balloons invariably do, this one began floating around the apartment at a height just above my head. Even stranger, it seemed to hover just behind me, wherever I went and at whatever pace. "This balloon is following me!" I told my husband the first day it happened. He laughed and put the balloon in the kitchen next to the garbage, saying, "Honey, you're nuts."

There was no laughter when we awakened the next morning. The balloon was hovering next to my side of the bed, just above my pillow. "Omigod," my husband muttered.

"Do you believe me now?" I said.

During the next three days, although I never touched it, that balloon followed me everywhere. When I came in the front door, it would travel from the living room ceiling to the hallway. It traveled with me into the kitchen as I cooked dinner and every time I went to the bathroom. My husband would say, "Hi, Bart," as the balloon floated behind my chair as we sat down at the dinner table. "Hi, Bart," my daughter would say as I leaned over to kiss her goodnight, the balloon bobbing next to her bed.

On the fourth day, the balloon became flatter and flatter, moved slower and slower, and floated lower and lower, finally sinking to the floor—at the front door. My eyes were wet. It was time.

"Thank you, Bart darling," I whispered as I put the deflated balloon outside for the super to pick up. "Thank you for visiting. It was a big help to me. I'm ready now to let you go."

—*Molly Gordy*

❦

Comment
If only for a fleeting moment, love scales even the great wall between life and death.

I could barely sleep. Dawn was almost breaking, but I had been up all night, tossing and turning and worrying myself sick over the baby I carried deep in my womb. Finally, as morning came, I confronted my deepest fears. *Something is definitely wrong,* I acknowledged to myself at last. *I must see the doctor immediately.*

I had hoped the doctor would pooh-pooh my fears and send me away with the gentle reassurance that everything was all right. Instead, his face reflected the despair I felt, and the news was bad.

"I'm so very sorry, Mrs. Gopin, but you are experiencing an early miscarriage."

I was silent.

In an awkward attempt to console me, he pressed on: "You know, 20 percent of all pregnancies end in miscarriage. These disappointments happen."

It was hard to absorb his words. My five previous pregnancies had all reached full term, so I had no reason to suspect that this one would be any different.

"You're still young . . . you'll have more children." The doctor was trying to be upbeat.

I went home and followed his instructions until the pain and discomfort increased. Later that day I was admitted to the hospital near my home. After several hours of pain and tension, I was examined again and told that the fetus had been discharged from my body.

It was all over.

I remained in the hospital until the next day, which was July 15, to make sure that my body was returning to normal. Just as I was filling out the documents that had to be completed before I could be formally discharged, I began talking to a woman nearby who was also intently filling out forms.

Sally had also had a miscarriage the day before. We didn't know each other, yet the opportunity to empathize with each other's sorrow was cathartic.

"The doctors say that the fetuses that we lose are usually severely deformed," Sally said. "So it really is a blessing that they don't have to be born only to undergo a life of constant physical pain and suffering."

"I know . . . but I still feel so empty inside," I responded sadly.

"I had my own expectations, too," Sally said, and then paused. "But I really do believe that even the pregnancies that we lose have a purpose in the divine plan."

As we were about to part, I suddenly exclaimed: "We'll meet each other again in 11 months. But not here—in the maternity wing!"

Sally smiled. I would have liked more time to talk, but my husband had arrived to take me home.

The following year, on June 13, which was almost exactly 11 months later, I gave birth to a healthy baby girl, delivered by a different doctor in a different hospital in a different city, an hour away from my home.

Just as I was getting out of bed several hours after the birth in order to visit my newborn in the nursery, I passed a familiar-looking woman in the corridor. Goose bumps broke out on my arms. It was Sally, the woman who had miscarried on the same day that I had in the hospital near my home. She too had switched to a new doctor affiliated with a different hospital, and she too had traveled an extra hour to have her baby—a boy, born here . . . two days earlier!

So we had met each other again, after all, but this time we shared our joy instead of our grief, both of us overwhelmed with gratitude that my personal prophecy had been fulfilled.

—*Sara Gopin*

✎

Comment

When the lips speak from the heart, a simple expression of empathy and encouragement can suddenly be transformed into words of prophecy.

It was the last half hour of her shift, and Lein Godfrey was tired. She waitressed two nights a week to supplement her income as a hairdresser, and both jobs required her to be on her feet.

The Saigon Restaurant in Madison, Wisconsin, was deserted. The "regulars"—who knew how punctilious the owner was about closing at precisely 10 P.M. had already vacated the premises, and Lein was busy cleaning up.

So when a stranger walked in at 9:30 and sat down at Lein's table, she sighed.

"Please," she asked another waitress at a different station, "can you take my table? I just want to clean up and get out of here."

The woman was usually accommodating, but that night she too was exhausted. "You take the table, Lein. Come on, you can do it."

Reluctantly, Lein approached the man. She brightened a little when she noticed that he looked as though he came from Vietnam. Even though the restaurant was billed as Vietnamese, many patrons who came to sample the food were just adventurous gourmands and had no connection to her native country. But this stranger definitely appeared to be a fellow countryman, and she never wasted an opportunity to press her search.

Every time Lein encountered a Vietnamese-looking man or woman, she always asked the same question, plain and outright: "Where are you from?"

It had been more than two decades since Lein had started asking strangers this question in the hope of unearthing her long-lost family in Vietnam. And for 20 years her question had yielded no results.

Now she was tired, exhausted, almost drained of the ability to speak. But the hope that still fluttered in her heart made her press on. "So," she said as she stood at the man's table, order pad in hand, "where are you from?"

In 1972, during the Vietnam War, Lein had left Vietnam in search of opportunities. Her departure was not a rejection of her family or of her culture, but simply a quest for a better life. She thought they would all eventually reunite, and she considered her leavetaking to be temporary. But circumstances rendered her actions permanent. The chaos that ensued in her country in the wake of the war, the turmoil and upheaval that prevailed, had left her as good as orphaned. She had never been able to reestablish contact with the family she left behind, nor locate them through the usual channels.

All these years, she had felt so alone.

In Madison, on her own, she had achieved many milestones, progressed through different stages: She had married, given birth, gotten divorced. And she had longed for someone close—a mother, a relative—to walk her through these events, counsel her, support her, hold her hand. But no one ever had. Even when she married, in a traditional wedding ceremony, there had been no one to stand at her side. In contrast, her husband had been encircled by crowds of beaming relatives.

The clients at the hairdressing salon where she worked were loyal to her, and her friends at church were kind. But none were family.

"So," she said again as she addressed the stranger, whose name was Phan Dat, "where are you from?"

"Maryland," he said, and her heart sank. "I'm in town for one day to do some medical research at the university," Phan Dat told her. "I'm staying downtown for the night."

Lein couldn't hide her surprise. "What made you come all the way to the West Side?" she asked. "We're so far from downtown."

"Well, I was looking for a Vietnamese restaurant and I found two listings in the phone book. One was for the 'I'm Here' Restaurant on Park Street, and the other was for this one."

"But the 'I'm Here' Restaurant is so much closer to downtown," Lein protested.

"You're right," Phan Dat said, shrugging. "I could've just walked there from my hotel, instead of driving here. I dunno. Something just made me come to this one instead. The name sounded good."

"So," she repeated, "where are you from . . . originally?"

"Saigon."

"Me, too," she said. "What part of Saigon?"

"Truong Minh Nahng," he answered.

"Me, too," Lein said, becoming excited. After 20 years, she had finally found someone from her area. "Did you ever know a man by the name of Le Hac?" she asked, trying to create some frame of reference.

"He's my uncle," the stranger replied.

"No, he's *my* uncle," Lein said.

Phan Dat and Lein Godfrey, they discovered, were *first cousins*.

Lein was frozen in shock. She couldn't believe the coincidence: Phan Dat was in town for one night; he had arbitrarily decided to travel across town to the Saigon Restaurant; and he had randomly chosen to sit at her table. She worked there only two nights a week, and a half hour later she would have been gone.

Phan Dat was also in a state of disbelief, but for other reasons. His uncle, Le Hac, was a rich, successful architect, renowned throughout Saigon, and he wondered whether Lein Godfrey might be some opportunistic, gold-digging phony. So he quizzed her relentlessly about family history and genealogy. When she answered all his questions to his satisfaction, he finally embraced her as one of his own.

Later, when they moved to a Denny's restaurant to continue their talk (the Saigon owner still insisted on closing at 10 P.M. despite the momentousness of their encounter), Lein discovered that tragedy had struck her immediate family. Her mother had died of heart disease in 1990 and her only brother had been killed in a Cambodian street fight. But much of her kin had emigrated to the United States, and she now knew their whereabouts. A dear aunt now resided in St. Louis, a cousin in Minneapolis. And there were more than two dozen members of her family currently living in several California cities, close enough to visit, with whom she could surely reconnect.

On February 2, 1997, Lein traveled to California to meet her long-lost family. Cousins who had been childhood playmates were now grown up and prosperous; once-indomitable uncles were now frail and blind. So much had changed over the years—there was, after all, a 22-year void.

But after initial suspicions were allayed and understandable skepticism vanquished, Lein was warmly welcomed back into the family fold. And even though her relatives lived far from Madison, Lein now feels that she has finally found the family and the support system she yearned for most of her life.

"This is the best thing that's happened to me," Lein says. "My son is my greatest gift, but you need your blood, too. I needed my family.

"There is a Vietnamese saying that when the leaf flies away from the tree, it is lost. I was the leaf and I flew back to be with the tree."

Comment
We are never lost to those who long for our return.

All through her childhood, Tanya Fisher was possessed by a vague disquiet—an uneasiness she could not pin down, a free-floating anxiety that simmered beneath the surface of her very normal, ordinary, happy life. Her father and mother, Fred and Hazel Smith, were devoted parents, and her upbringing was typical in every respect. Still . . . something was missing; something was not quite right. Tanya didn't feel the bond with them that she supposed other children felt with their parents. Somewhere deep inside of her, a little voice whispered that she was not in the family into which she had been born.

When Tanya was nine, two momentous events in her life occurred. She heard the word "adoption" casually mentioned in someone's conversation and learned, for the first time, what it meant. And her family moved to a new neighborhood in Winston-Salem, North Carolina.

Tanya felt electricity course through her body when awareness of the meaning of adoption first dawned on her. "That's it, then!" she breathed in relief, having finally found the word that described the disquiet she had felt all those years. "I must be adopted!"

Dim memories of having been with a different family the first four years of her life swam up to her consciousness. But when she confronted her parents, they chastised her sternly. "We are your natural parents and don't you ever speak of this again!"

And she never did.

She ached, but Tanya was an obedient child, so she squelched her yearning to know the truth. But at least she found some semblance of relief through one outlet: Her lifelong wish to forge a genuine and heartfelt bond with an adult had finally been fulfilled. The new next-door neighbor, an elderly woman with a warm smile and an attentive ear, demonstrated genuine interest in Tanya, and they visited with each other often. Tanya was drawn to her, and they talked all the time. At last, Tanya had forged a meaningful connection.

When Tanya was 22, engaged to be married, and needed a copy of her birth certificate as required by law, the truth emerged.

The qualms and doubts that had besieged her in her youth had not been unfounded, after all. Every day of misgiving, every night of apprehension, was finally confirmed as being legitimate and real. Tanya had been adopted, just as she had always suspected.

"Can you tell me the name of my birth mother?" she begged the clerk at County Records. But the state's strict privacy laws made it impossible for the official to disclose the details. "No, I can't do that," the woman responded brusquely.

Tanya was not daunted. She was determined to find her biological mother, no matter what the odds.

Her first break came four years later, when a sympathetic clerk took pity on her. Making an elaborate show of examining the records, the clerk voicelessly turned them around so that they faced Tanya and she could read the name clearly stamped on the document: G. L. Truesdale. Her mother!

Detective work revealed that G. L. Truesdale was now Gwen Davis, also residing in Winston-Salem. She worked at the Water Department, and it was there that Tanya first contacted her.

"Good afternoon—City Utilities," Gwen sang out when she picked up the phone one December, blissfully unaware that her life was about to change.

"Does Gwen Davis work there?" the caller asked.

"Yes, this is she."

The caller hung up. Tanya, trembling at the momentousness of her call and fearful of its outcome, had a bad case of cold feet.

Then the phone rang again, and once more, the caller asked about Gwen Davis. But hearing her biological mother's very real and live voice on the phone made Tanya freeze in shock and panic, and she hung up a second time.

She worked again to gather her courage, to summon the nerve. On the third try, Tanya finally made contact. "Gwen Davis?" she asked bravely. "This is Tanya Smith Fisher. I was given up for adoption . . ."

On the other end, Gwen screamed.

Her heart fluttering, Tanya paused, trying to decipher the meaning of that scream. *Was that a good scream,* she asked herself, *a thrilled-beyond-belief scream, an I'm-delirious-with-happiness-scream, or is it an annoyed, frightened, I-don't-want-you-in-my-life scream?*

Tanya wasn't sure. She didn't know how to proceed. Finally, she asked in a small, quiet voice, "Are you mad?"

"Mad?" Gwen Davis shouted, incredulous. "I could never be mad at you. When can I see you?"

"You can see me *today*," Tanya said.

She went to Gwen's office straight from work, wondering what kind of welcome awaited her. Gwen held out her arms to Tanya and cried: "Just hold me, hold me!"

The very words that Tanya had waited a lifetime to hear.

That night, Gwen took Tanya to her home to meet her two brothers and get started on 27 years of catching up.

Gwen explained that she had been only 15—"just a child myself"—when she had given birth to Tanya. "I didn't know what was happening. As soon as you were born, they came and took you from me. I started crying and that was the last time I saw you. I was sure that I would never see you again. But all through my life, I thought about you often, wondering how you were, and praying to God that you were happy and well."

That first evening, they all began their catching up. They exchanged little tidbits of information about their respective lives and tried to fill in the empty spaces that yawned between them with details, data, concrete facts.

"So where did you actually grow up?" Gwen asked Tanya eagerly.

"Oh, on 24th Street," Tanya answered in an offhand manner.

Gwen gazed at her in disbelief.

"Twenty-fourth Street!" she exclaimed. "I lived on 24th Street too! What was your address?"

And then the truth emerged. Tanya had grown up in a brick house on 24th Street one house away from Gwen. They had lived on the same block at the same time, and neither of them had had a clue who the other really was.

And the woman next door whom Tanya visited often and with whom she had forged a deep bond?

"I never thought anything of it," Gwen muses; "Momma just liked little girls. . . ." It was Tanya's *own grandmother*.

"Momma's gone now," says Gwen, "but I'll always believe that deep inside her heart she knew that this little girl was her grandchild. . . . It's just a miracle that God sent her back to me."

Gwen and Tanya have had no problem in picking up the pieces and relating to one another now as mother and daughter. They've fallen into the roles naturally, and the 27-year gap gets narrower each day.

"My mother is my best friend," Tanya reflects.

"I love Tanya with all my heart and if I had to do it again, I'd have raised her," says Gwen. "I never want her to go out of my life again."

❧

Comment
When souls are joined, bodies must reunite.

$\mathcal{I}n$ 1992, I advertised for a husband in the personal-ads section of a local Boston newspaper.

I was pleased with my initiative, gratified that I was not being passive but rather was being proactive about my single status. But all that my action achieved was a series of bad dates and no chemistry. With my optimism dampened after several months of disappointing dead ends, I finally canceled my ad.

I guess I'll meet my future husband some other way, I concluded.

I was sure that my soul mate would eventually show up, but I was 33 at the time, my biological clock was ticking, and I was scared and impatient. I was also tired of suffering through awkward dates with men who sounded terrific on the telephone and in their letters, but who were a whole different story when encountered in person. As soon as I met them, I usually wanted to head straight for home—fast!

It turns out that the man of my dreams was married at the time my ads were running, and he was not a subscriber to this local newspaper, anyway. But months later, when his marriage fell apart, he reluctantly reentered the singles scene. He happened to visit an aunt in another town, who gave him her current copy of the local newspaper, suggesting that he check out the personal-ads section. When Stephen glanced at the personals column for that week, he saw an ad that immediately grabbed his attention. He wrote to the mystery lady that night.

That ad was *mine*. But how was this possible? I had canceled my ad *months earlier*. By apparent coincidence, the newspaper had erroneously reentered my ad in the *one and only* personal-ads page Stephen had ever read, long after I had canceled my order.

Stephen and I met the very night I received his letter. He knew instantly that he wanted to marry me. Since his divorce wasn't yet final, it took me a few weeks to come to the same conclusion. Stephen warmed up my cold feet in a short time; his divorce was finalized; and we were married a year after our first date.

I called the local newspaper to tell them of our good news and to ask how my ad had ended up back in the newspaper—without my knowledge or permission— months after I had canceled it. My immediate assumption, when I saw the ad, had been that they were having a slow month and had put in some old ads just to fill out the classified section. My hypothesis, however, was wrong.

Courtney, the employee who handled the personals each week and took my call, knew immediately who I was. She was baffled by my query and responded in genuine surprise. "But I distinctly remember you calling me and telling me to rerun your ad on Labor Day weekend," she insisted.

When I heard her statement, I got a chill. "But it's not true," I protested. "I never called you. How can this be?"

We both fell silent as we contemplated the mystery. I was shocked and amazed. "Oh, well," I said lightly, "it must have been my guardian angel!"

To this day, I still don't know who made that call. But it was a true blessing that the "mistake" was made, because I'm married as a result.

—Azriela Jaffe

*F*or decades, Abigail Van Buren, the woman behind the venerable and beloved "Dear Abby" advice column, has helped the love-lorn, the strife-torn, and the forlorn. Her wisdom and counsel have been a source of strength and succor for the millions of fans who follow her column faithfully, a column that is syndicated in countless newspapers across the United States. As such, it is probably no exaggeration to state that in many cases, Abby's advice has literally changed lives.

In 1995, elementary schoolteacher Brenda Fredricksen, a 24-year-old devoted fan of the advice columnist, was reading "Dear Abby" as she regularly did, when she was struck by a plea inserted in that day's edition. *The holidays are approaching,* Abby gently reminded her readers, *and our servicemen and women overseas are so lonely. It's easy to be swept up by our own whirlwind of business, but let's try to remember them, too. A card or note from their fellow Americans at home would be a special way to let them know they are not forgotten.*

Brenda's heart opened as she thought of how bleak the holidays must be for servicemen overseas. Alone, isolated in a foreign country, separated from loved ones at the most meaningful time of the year . . . she shuddered at the thought of their solitariness. She resolved to follow Abby's advice that very afternoon. *It's the least I can do,* she thought.

"Just wanted you to know there are people thinking about you," she wrote on a greeting card that she addressed to "Any Soldier." She sincerely hoped that her note would uplift the recipient's spirits, whomever he or she might prove to be.

Thousands of miles away at an army base in Korea, Private Michael Johnson avidly awaited mail call. He relished, indeed yearned for any word from home, and when he was offered a random letter from a sack marked "Operation Abby," he accepted the envelope gratefully. Any mail, even mail from anonymous Americans who had written at Abby's behest, was a welcome reprieve from the loneliness that enwrapped him.

Michael was touched by the warmth Brenda's note exuded. Impulsively, he decided to write her back. *She sounds like such a nice person,* he thought. "People like you keep us going," he wrote. He also told her a little bit about himself and the unit he was in.

Brenda had never expected to receive a response from "Any Soldier," and she was intrigued to learn that the person who had randomly gotten her card was in the 82nd Airborne.

"My dad was in the 82nd Airborne, too," Brenda wrote back to Michael, feeling that they now shared some common ground, some sense of connection, as a result. But her father had died when she was only four, she told him, and she poured out her feelings of loss in a fresh and honest way.

Michael had also experienced a loss—but a more recent one, one that still hurt. Encouraged by Brenda's openness in her second letter to him, Michael's own return note also spoke honestly of his painful breakup with his ex-girlfriend. Although geographically far apart, their letters bridged the distance with their warmth and candor.

Things accelerated from there. They exchanged pictures, then e-mails, and finally, long-distance phone calls. The sense that they had both had about each other in the initial round of correspondence was validated, and getting stronger every day.

But would the sizzle of the correspondence translate into great chemistry in person?

It would. It did.

"It was just like a movie," Brenda sighs of their first meeting four months later. On the second date, Michael proposed, and by the end of that very weekend, they were married.

As an advice columnist, Abigail Van Buren wears many hats—marriage counselor, child psychologist, and social worker are just a few of the functions she performs in everyday life—but this may very well be the first case where she has unwittingly served as . . . matchmaker!

❧

Comment

A ripple of kindness radiating from one side of the world can generate a tidal wave of love and gratitude on the other.

*M*y office was a festive place, where we celebrated each other's good fortune with a joy rarely seen in more competitive environments. Hardly a week went by that we didn't toast someone's award, promotion, engagement, or birthday. Usually I was delighted that my desk was located next to the only counter, so that the refreshments and celebrants invariably landed near me.

But not on that particular day. I hadn't confided to anyone at work that I had suffered six miscarriages. But as I watched the pile of baby gifts accumulate for Sally from Advertising on her last day before maternity leave, I didn't have to. As the receptionist placed a diaper-shaped cake on the counter next to me, my anguish was so obvious that my boss, catching sight of me, leaned over and whispered, "Molly, take a slide. I don't want to see you back here until tomorrow."

There are myriad options for women who suffer from infertility, but not for those who can conceive at the drop of a hat, but never make it to the finish line. "Just keep trying," the doctors would say, and my husband and I would regard each other bleakly, wondering if we could bear to spend another three or four months trying in vain not to get too attached to the potential child growing inside me—only to mourn in private for yet another loss.

"Help me to align my will with thy will, Oh Lord," I prayed each night as I tried to keep the faith. Eventually, however, I became obsessed with my inability to join the community of parents. Every time I went grocery shopping, to the park, out to eat, or on the bus or subway, all I could see were babies in strollers pushed by beaming mommies. I slept fitfully, wondering why I couldn't attain what had come so easily to my mother and sister. I knew that self-pity would only deepen my depression, but try as I might, I could not escape a growing feeling of resentment one more miscarriage later. So, it was in a sullen spirit that I approached the Jewish New Year in 1988, after my seventh miscarriage, at the age of 35.

In the Jewish religion, services follow a set procedure that parallels the lunar calendar. The Torah— the books of Genesis, Exodus, Leviticus, Numbers, and Deuteronomy—is divided into weekly portions that are read and discussed at exactly the same time each year. This is cause for some consternation among those Jews who only attend synagogue on major holidays, for they hear only the same passages discussed year after year.

Chief among these is the portion read at Rosh Hashona, the Jewish New Year. For 30 years, I had sat through countless New Year's sermons analyzing the chapter in Genesis where God asks Abraham to sacrifice Isaac, his beloved son. This year, I sat lost in my own thoughts, until the rabbi began reading the portion that came after that, about a barren woman named Hannah. So great was Hannah's grief, the story goes, that the prophet Elijah thought she was drunk when he encountered her on a mountaintop praying that God grant her a child. When he learned the truth, Elijah gave Hannah a special blessing, promising her that one year later, she would give birth to a son whom she must raise as a special child of God. Hannah agreed, and the baby grew up to be the prophet Samuel.

As the rabbi spoke, this story I had heard so many times before with indifference pierced me like a lightning bolt, and I fled the sanctuary, sobbing. Sitting down in a deserted stairwell underneath the exit sign, I poured out all my rage at God. "Tell me," I prayed, "what has Hannah got that I haven't got? Why do you deny me this, when I, too, promise to offer to do my best to educate my child to love and serve you?"

There was no immediate reply. No prophets appeared; no thunder split the sky; I felt no presence comforting me. But in February, my husband and I conceived again, and this time, for some reason, it took. On October 2, 1989, I waddled into Rosh Hashona services seven months pregnant. But this time I would not be able to hear the end of the sermon either. My waters broke, and I was rushed to the hospital to give birth prematurely.

The baby was so tiny that she got tangled in her umbilical cord and choked until her heart and breathing stopped. She was delivered by emergency cesarean section and brought back to life by a gifted team of doctors exactly one year to the day after I had prayed for a child. We named her Eliana—a Hebrew phrase meaning "God answered me." She remained in the hospital for eight days and we brought her home on Yom Kippur—the Day of Atonement, which is the holiest day on the Jewish calendar.

"I don't know about you, but I don't need a billboard to get the message here," I told my husband. "One way or another, we are going to send this child to religious day school."

This was an easy vow to make in the passion of the moment, but harder to keep as years went by. When it came time for our beloved child to enter kindergarten, we lacked the funds to pay for private school. We were a whopping $6,000 short of paying the tuition at a school that, at the time, had no scholarship fund. My husband was sanguine. "Look, if it's not meant to be, it's not meant to be," he said. "We'll send her to Sunday school."

I, on the other hand, was troubled. It was Friday, and I went to synagogue for Sabbath services and said a second prayer, this time more humbly. "Dear God," I prayed, "please send me a sign that shows me what I should do. I'm trying to keep the promise I made to you. If you want me to go in another direction, that's fine, but if this is what you want from me, I beg you, please send me a sign."

I left the service feeling strangely comforted. As I arrived home, my husband met me at the door, waving a cordless telephone excitedly. "It's my brother calling!" he said. "He says the lawyer made a mistake in our father's estate, and we're each owed $6,000!"

Not $5,000, or $4,000, but exactly the amount of the missing tuition. "Eli-Ana"—God had answered me again.

—*Molly Gordy*

৽৽৽৽

Comment

As we circle through life, coming upon the same sights and sounds again and again, an old familiar seed finally takes root, and something new is born in us.

It was the spring of '42 and they were two kids living on two continents when pen and paper—and a school assignment—brought them together.

She was 14, a student in Miss Frady's class, when the eighth-graders were asked to select a pen pal from a list of kids in England. It was a small way of uniting teens during the war.

He was 14, too, a grocery errand boy outside London, when he began writing her.

They had little in common. She was a fresh-faced girl who rarely strayed far from her father's farm. He was a war-weary boy who dreamed of traveling the world even as he hunkered down in a dark, drafty bomb shelter.

But the two found enough to write about for years.

When the war ended and he was in the Royal Navy, he wrote to say that he wanted to visit her in Iowa. She told her fiancé, who quickly laid down the law. No more letters.

It seemed the pen pals would never cross paths again.

Dear Sir or Madam,
I am writing to see if you can help me in my plight.
During the war years, I was writing to a girl as a pen friend.
Her name was then Miss Colleen Lee. . . . If you could by any chance trace her for me, I would be very grateful.
Yours truly,
Geoffrey W. Lake

The letter was dated October 19, 1989, and now, almost 10 years later, Geoffrey still can't say precisely why he decided to look up his old pen pal.

He was 61, happily married for decades to his wife, Eileen, with a grown son, Michael. But something tugged at the retired factory worker.

He didn't remember Colleen's address, but couldn't forget her hometown's distinctive name. So he addressed the envelope:

The Mayor's Parlor
Soldier, Iowa

With just 250 souls in Soldier, there are no strangers. It turned out the mayor and Colleen were good friends. She was now Colleen Straight, having long ago married her childhood sweetheart, Harvey.

Geoffrey and Eileen were planning to visit the United States when his note arrived in Soldier.

"I've got this letter from some fellow in England," the mayor told Colleen.

She smiles as she remembers that day: "I knew right away who it was."

Dear Geoff,
What a surprise! I believe it's 45 years since we corresponded . . .

Where to begin? Colleen dashed off a breezy three-page letter describing her family and where they had lived over the years. She also invited Geoffrey and Eileen to Soldier.

And she signed off:

Your pen pal, Colleen

Back in Waltham Abbey, Geoffrey was thrilled.

And so they began corresponding again. They shared over-the-fence tidbits about daily life. They always signed their letters as couples. Colleen and Harvey. Eileen and Geoff. There was no romance. "It was a friendship all the way through," Geoffrey says.

Then in December 1992, Colleen had sad news.

"This is not an easy letter to write," she confided. "I lost Harvey . . . I know I must not dwell on his passing, but I do think of it a lot."

Geoffrey responded with a condolence card and one each year on the anniversary of Harvey's death.

Geoffrey and Eileen's plans to visit Colleen fell through, but the letters continued.

Then in November 1997, Geoffrey's wife of 45 years died. This time, Colleen did the consoling.

Dear Geoff and Michael:
It's difficult at this sad time to find the right words to comfort you. You will find yourself thinking of all the things you have done together and that helps a lot. . . . Just be thankful you had a good life together.

On a January night in 1998, a downcast Geoffrey dialed his phone. He was tempted to hang up before a little girl answered in a cozy living room 4,300 miles away.

"Grandmother, somebody I can't understand wants to talk to you," 10-year-old Ashley said, handing Colleen the receiver.

"Hello, Colleen, do you know who this is?" the caller asked. His accent gave him away.

For the first time in 56 years, the childhood correspondents spoke to one another.

"After hearing his voice, I think I felt he was real," Colleen says.

They talked for a while and at the end, Colleen recalls, "He said, 'Good-bye, love.' I really took that to heart. I thought, Boy . . . he means business! But that's just an everyday phrase in England."

Still, she says, "It sort of melted my heart."

Geoffrey wanted to visit her, though Colleen felt it was too soon for the new widower. So she delicately put him off.

But their calls and letters picked up. Their words became more tender, their thoughts more intimate.

"We more or less . . . ," Geoffrey begins.

". . . struck up a romance," Colleen finishes his sentence.

Still, the two had never even spent an hour together.

"We talked about maybe we wouldn't like one another at all," Colleen says. "We had no idea what our temperaments would really be like. You can't tell that by letter writing."

Still, he persisted and finally she agreed to meet him.

> *My darling Colleen,*
> *It sounds a bit ridiculous the way we feel about one another. Here we are, both approaching the age of 70 and carrying on as though we are teenagers but honey, I've got a young heart and cannot express my feelings any other way. I love it and I love you, honey.*
> *Roll on May 28!*

That was the date they agreed to meet in New York. The appointed place was the customs desk at Kennedy Airport. Geoffrey said he'd be carrying a Tesco bag (the name of a British supermarket). Inside was a bottle of champagne and a fruitcake the former Navy chef had made to woo her with his baking talents.

When Colleen's plane was three and a half hours late, Geoffrey worried that he had been stood up. Then he saw a five-foot woman with short brown hair approaching. He recognized the bejeweled denim outfit she had described. She spotted the Tesco bag.

"Our eyes met," Colleen says. "We embraced."

"It was love at first sight," Geoffrey says.

They spent three days touring New York before heading to Iowa, where he met her family. Everything clicked. There was no tension, no awkwardness.

In no time, Geoffrey decided to move to Iowa. He returned home to settle some personal matters, then last September on his first night back, he bent on one knee and proposed.

"I said yes!" she recalls, turning to Geoffrey as they sit at the kitchen table. "I didn't even stop to think about it, did I?"

He leans in, quietly offering his own recollection: "Teary-eyed, she was."

Two flags—the Stars and Stripes and the Union Jack—flutter outside the white-frame house at the end of the road.

Inside, Geoffrey, wearing an Iowa Hawkeyes sweatshirt, marvels at the turn of events.

"A half-century and we're together again—well, not again, we're now together," he says.

"It seems like a fairly tale," Colleen says. "People say it was just meant to be. And we're both happier for it."

"More than happy," Geoffrey adds.

On November 28, 1998, the wartime pen pals became husband and wife. They sent out word to friends and family:

A reception honoring the newlyweds, Colleen and Geoff, will be held on Saturday . . .

It was their first joint correspondence.

❧

Comment

When old friendship blossoms into romance, winter releases the sweetness and promise of spring.

I woke up in horror in the middle of the night with sweat pouring off my body. The dream had been so real that I had to pinch myself to realize that I was awake and that it hadn't really happened. I felt an immense weight on my chest, as if I had been sobbing and couldn't get a breath.

I had dreamed that my dad had been in a terrible accident. I could clearly see the waiting room at the hospital. It was strange, because I could see my mother and stepmother sitting together. I remember thinking that it couldn't possibly be happening, because in real life they would *never* sit together. In my dream, Dad—my mentor, my confidant, my port in every storm—died, and I felt this horrible emptiness because I hadn't hugged him for a while.

Dad was a reserved, undemonstrative man who shared his love in quiet, thoughtful ways. He was always telling bad jokes and bragging about how healthy he was. I realized I hadn't given him a hug for a long time— too long. The achy, lonely, and sad feeling persisted until morning, when I was finally able to give him a call. It was such a joy to hear his cheerful "hello."

Immediate relief flooded my tense body. I said, "You have to come visit me today. I'll tell you about it when you get here." He was puzzled, but decided to come on his lunch hour. I waited anxiously until I heard his motorcycle pull up. There was the 53-year-old, trim, business-suited, baldheaded "kid" as he hopped off his new toy.

When Dad came through the door, I hugged him as I've never hugged anyone before. As I held Dad, I felt joy that he was alive and that I was actually touching him. At the same time, I remembered the dream and the experience of sadness and horror that had engulfed me. It was a feeling that I couldn't shake off, and I realized I was trembling. Dad and I looked sadly at each other as I told him about my dream.

It was on a beautiful Saturday morning several months later that I got the phone call. Dad had been in a motorcycle accident and had a "few broken ribs." I called my family and rushed to the hospital, where I was allowed into his room. The shock was almost more than I could bear, and tears welled up in my eyes.

Dad was lying with his eyes closed. He had a large gash on his forehead, and some of his teeth were missing. He had a tube running into his nose and down into his abdomen, and there was blood flowing from the tube into a large bottle on the floor. Although he looked horrible, the doctor assured me that he appeared much worse than he actually was. The injuries he had sustained, the doctor told me, were a few broken ribs and slight liver damage, nothing more.

Dad recognized my voice when I whispered his name, and he told me about the accident and about the woman who had hit him. "Tell her that I forgive her. She didn't mean to hit me," he said, as he arched his back in excruciating pain.

I was more condemning than he. I felt utter fury at this woman who had run a stop sign and hit my dad with her car.

As we talked, Dad's condition suddenly worsened and he was rushed into surgery. As his gurney was wheeled past me in the corridor, I grabbed his hand and told him I loved him. As I entered the visitors' lounge to begin the interminable process of waiting, I saw my mother and stepmother sitting together with most of my family. Four hours later, we were called in to see Dad. He had just gotten out of surgery, had a tube down his throat, and had a white pallor.

He died only minutes later. My dear, beloved dad was gone.

When I had first experienced my dream months before, it was as if I were peering into a window at the future. I felt I had been prepared for Dad's death in order to make our relationship complete. When Dad died, I felt a strange peacefulness, because I had been given a second chance—a chance to hug him, to have deep discussions with him about life, death, and God, and about my own aspirations for the future. The circle had been closed.

Afterwards, I was tormented by thoughts of Dad's accident. I imagined him moments after he had been hit, lying in the street, alone and in pain. I wondered how long he had had to wait until the ambulance came. My anger at the woman who hit him swelled. Had she been drunk? What right did she have to drive . . . and kill my dad? But Dad's final words haunted me: "Tell her that I forgive her. She didn't mean to hit me."

Dad had asked me to be his messenger, and how could I refuse his deathbed request? I finally found the strength to write the woman and convey Dad's last message of absolution. In the letter, I also faced my grief and asked the questions that had obsessed me for so long. How exactly had it happened? What made her plow into my dad? Was he conscious after he had been hit? Had he said anything of significance?

I was surprised when I received a phone call from her in response. She answered all my questions through anguish and tears. She herself was a nurse, had had a very sick child in the car, and was on her way to the doctor. She had halted at the stop sign and then continued driving. She suddenly felt her car hit something and thought it was a dog. When she went to look, she found Dad. She put his head into her lap as he gently squeezed her hand. As we talked, I felt an inner peace. Dad was dead, but his love, forgiveness, and kindness still lived on.

When my sister Diane returned to Louisiana after Dad's funeral, she found a letter in her mailbox that he had written the night before he died, and out slipped a copy of a poem that he had sent along.

Life is worth living
Wherever you are
Deep down in a dungeon
Or high on a star.

Life is worth living
It all has a plan.
When God knows you're giving
The best that you can.

The Saint and the Sinner
The great and the small
We are all God's children
And he loves us all.

So pray when you're happy
And pray when you're blue
For life is worth living
When God lives with you.

—Nick Kenny

—Patricia Minch

$\mathcal{I}$t is at twilight that I remember Mama best. I can still see her chasing fireflies, her skirt swinging below her knees. As the fading sun slips behind Georgia pine trees, it leaves the sky blanketed with a sunburst of orange. A glow radiates from Mama's face and laughter dances in her hazel eyes as she gathers fireflies in her hand and shows them to me.

Until I was about five, Mama caught fireflies and put them, still blinking, into an empty mayonnaise jar. Later, she tucked me into bed and I pretended those pulsating little bugs were a nightlight. Sometimes, they even seemed to be winking at me.

Even at that young age, I was painfully aware Mama never once told me she loved me. It troubled me that she never kissed me good night or at any other time, for that matter. But I knew she cared; she just showed it in a unique way—through humor. I remember her humor being especially poignant as she battled lung cancer. In 1980, Mama began experiencing chest pains. After a few days of pain so severe she had trouble talking, she let me drive her to the doctor.

Once in the examining room, Mama pulled the white paper gown over her head as she was instructed. She held the paper out for my inspection. "I hate these things," she said, a sparkle of mischief growing in her eyes. "I feel like an overgrown paperdoll." That was Mama. Though deeply concerned, I laughed out loud.

Later, the x-rays confirmed there was a tumor in her left lung. I had hoped it wasn't malignant but after a biopsy, the results came back positive. The doctor gave her a year to live.

During that year, Mama battled the cancer by staying busy. With my husband's help, she planted a small garden outside her mobile home on the south side of Atlanta. As soon as the sun blinked upon the horizon each morning, Mama dragged her three-legged stool outside and sat among the green beans, tomatoes, and cucumbers to weed the garden blossoming with life. After a half hour in the blazing sun, perspiration beaded her forehead and upper lip. She'd come in gasping.

Once, with the familiar twinkle in her eyes, she said, "You know, my breath keeps coming in short pants." Then she laughed. I knew what she was imagining — puffs of air dressed in a pair of short pants.

In April of 1981, Mama lay in a hospital bed, her long battle almost at an end. One day after radiation therapy, the nurse wheeled Mama's gurney back into her room. Although a shell of her former self, there was a smile twinkling in those hazel eyes. "My mouth is so dry," she said, "I thought they'd have to shave my tongue." Not only did I laugh out loud but the nurse smiled as well. Thankfully, Mama's humor made accepting her illness a little easier.

One day as I left the hospital room, I couldn't hold back the tears. I felt a comforting touch on my shoulder as I neared the nurse's station. I turned to see a nurse whose eyes showed deep concern. "Why can't you cry with your mother?" she asked. I shook my head trying to regain composure. "It's a shame," she went on, "because every time you leave, your mother cries, too."

I wanted so much to let Mama know I cared, but it was impossible since I'd never received outward affection from her. I simply didn't know how to show her I loved her. As I pondered our lives together, questions formed in my mind. Why can't I tell my mother I love her? Was it because of the betrayal I felt when she left my father? Perhaps it was Mama's growing alcoholism. Maybe she just couldn't handle love and was incapable of giving it. I didn't know. I only knew that I couldn't address my love for her with the words she couldn't say. I couldn't even kiss her.

With the rebirth of spring and the resurrection of the once-dormant azaleas and dogwoods, I found myself thinking of the true meaning of Easter. Although I was alienated from God during this season of sorrow, I remember pleading with Him, please help me say good-bye to my mother before it's too late. Every day I brought my barely used Bible to Mama's room and curled up on a vinyl chair partially hidden behind the hospital bed. One evening when twilight shadows filled the room, I sat in my usual place silently reading from the Psalms.

I don't know who the dark-haired nurse was who interrupted my thoughts, and she had no idea I was sitting there in the shadows. I held my breath as she walked up to Mama. Watching in silence, I saw the nurse gently brush Mama's chestnut hair from her face. She held Mama's face in her hands in the most tender way. I knew she must be an angel sent by God because she did the one thing I couldn't. She leaned down and kissed Mama's forehead. As I gently exhaled, the woman tiptoed from the room.

The next day doctors were forced to increase the dosage of morphine to ease Mama's pain. Through the veil of drugs, Mama's eyes glazed and I feared I had waited too late to say good-bye. Beneath the green oxygen mask, she struggled for every breath. I struggled with her. She probably won't hear me, I thought, but I have to tell her.

I picked up my mother's spindly hand and held it. I took a sharp breath, and for all the times I couldn't speak, I whispered, "Mama, I love you." For a heartbeat in eternity, Mama's eyes cleared. She looked at me and a smile traced her lips. The presence of God in that room was inexplicable. It was as though God Himself winked at me—like fireflies wink at children on warm, summer nights.

Nanette Thorsen-Snipes

$\mathcal{I}t$ was many years ago, but Lorelei Nachin would never forget how scared she felt the day she came to live at St. Peter's Orphanage in Manchester, New Hampshire. The big building filled with strangers terrified the five-year-old—that is, until she made her first friend.

"Do you want to play?" an older girl, Pat Arnold, asked Lorelei one day.

Lorelei said yes, and from that day on, the girls were inseparable.

But after nine years, the time came for Pat to leave the orphanage, and later Lorelei left, too. Both women were soon married and living in other states, yet a day didn't go by without Pat or Lorelei thinking of her friend. But when they checked with New Hampshire City Hall, they were told that the records were sealed.

It seemed they'd never see each other again—until one day, 43 years later . . .

Lorelei, now 56, was driving near her Florida home when she pulled into a restaurant for lunch. Before long, she found herself chatting with a man who was sitting at a table across from her.

"Where are you from?" he asked.

"I grew up in Manchester, New Hampshire," Lorelei said. And for some reason, she even gave the address: 300 Kelley Street.

At that, a woman at the next table stood up. "Isn't that St. Peter's Orphanage?" she asked. "What's your name?"

Lorelei's heart began to race. "Lorelei," she answered.

"Lorelei Manning?" the woman gasped. "I'm Pat Arnold!"

"Pat!" Lorelei cried. "I can't believe it!"

It turned out that Pat, now 61, had just moved to Florida. "So many times through the years, I wanted to see you again!" Pat cried.

"Me, too!" Lorelei wept, throwing her arms around her old friend.

Today, the women get together as often as they can, and the bond they once felt is back—as strong as ever.

"Having Lorelei back in my life feels like a hole in my heart has been healed," Pat says.

Lorelei agrees: "Now that Pat is here, I think anything is possible. It's like I have my sister back."

—*Jamie Kiffel*

Permissions

Grateful acknowledgment is made to the following for permission to reprint previously published material:

"Angel on Wheels" by Julie B. Gibson reproduced with permission from Heroic Stories.com.

"Take the Time" by Barbara Deal and "I'll Share My Son with You," by Evelyn Myer Allison in the collection *Angels, Miracles & Messages — A Guideposts Book*. Copyright ©1996 by Thomas Nelson Publishers, Nashville, Tenn.

"Fate Brought These Friends Back Together" and "A Lost and Found Miracle for Hazel" by Peg Verone, October 10, 1999. Reprinted with permission from *Woman's World Magazine*, Englewood Cliffs, NJ.

"Her Prayer is Answered" by Christi Connor. Copyright ©1995 by Atlanta-Journal Constitution. Reproduced with permission of ATLANTA JOUR-CONSTITUTION in the format Trade Book via Copyright Clearance Center.

"Lessons in Emunah" edited by Naomi Mauer. Copyright ©March 5, 1999, *The Jewish Press*.

"A Sign for Our Times" and "A Promise on Mother's Day" by Joan Wester Anderson in the collection *Where Miracles Happen: True Stories of Heavenly Encounters*. Copyright ©1994 by Joan Wester Anderson. Published by Brett Books, Inc.

"Stitches in Time" by Roberta Messner. Reprinted with permission from *Guideposts Magazine* (January 1996) Copyright ©1995 by Guideposts, Carmel, NY 10512.

"Wartime Pen Pals Become Mates 56 Years Later," originally published in *The Times Union*, Feb. 14, 1999. Reprinted with permission from The Associated Press. Copyright ©1999.

Excerpt from *Waycross Herald Journal*, Waycross, GA by Larry Purdom, copyright ©1997.

Acknowledgments

There's lots of controversy swirling around the Internet these days, but I have to confess: it's where I've found the nicest friends! Kudos and everlasting thanks to Michael Powers (Thunder27), whose inspiring newsletter is a constant source of strength. He is an endless well of good cheer, kindness, warmth, and support. Azriela Jaffe, ECS newsletter founder and editor, is an amazing woman who truly embodies the word "friend." Meg Lundstrom, author of a phenomenal book called *The Power of Flow* has been especially generous. Minister John Sloat of the *Spiritual Bridge* Web site was a valuable resource. Editor Jennifer Basye Sanders first connected with me on the Web, and later sent me an invaluble lead that resulted in a story contained in these pages.

Over the last two years, a woman whom I knew only as "Inez" constantly sent me sweet, inspiring stories. In return, I sent her little notes of appreciation. I was always thrilled by her generosity of spirit and cheerful, loving attitude. One sad day, I received an e-mail from her family. Inez had passed away after a long, lingering illness that had lasted many years. All this time, she had been deathly sick, and I never knew. She had spent her days propped up in a wheelchair, her laptop computer her only lifeline to humanity. Despite her illness, despite her ominous prognosis, she devoted the last years of her life to performing random acts of loving kindness over the Web. I will miss her and her sweet, loving letters very much.

Everything in life is a vessel for both good and bad: It is up to us to decide how we want to harness our power. Inez used the Web to connect with people in a meaningful way. And that is exactly what we have always hoped to do with the *Small Miracles* series. May God bless you, our wonderful readers, with *many* miracles—both large and small—throughout your lives. You deserve them!

This book is as much my family's as my own: my husband Motty, and my sons Yossi and Eli. Love also to my sister, Miriam, my brother Moishe, and mother Claire. My friends are my blessings in my life: Anna Dinnah, Raizy, Yidis, Pessy, Bella, Annette, Babshi, Etta, Ruchama, Shulamis, Sora Laya, Tammy, Hindy, and Naomi Mauer. Noreen, Rose, and Minnie at Harnik's Happy House in Brooklyn—you guys are the greatest! We would also like to acknowledge the folks at Adams who have worked so hard on this book: Virginia Rubins, Linda Spencer, Wayne Jackson, Nancy True, Carrie Lewis, Bob Adams, and Pam Liflander.

—Yitta Halberstam

Among the many miracles of life are the special people with whom we travel. I would like to acknowledge my family, who have been loving and supportive of my efforts. My daughters, Arielle and Shira who fill me with joy. My dear husband Jules who has shown me the greatest miracle of all, the miracle of love.

I also want to thank the following people for their support, guidance, and friendship: Pesi Dinnerstein, Deena and Chet Edelman, Eta and Reuven Ansel, Ruchama and Yisrael Feuerman, Anna Ashton, Ruth Wolfert, David Krauss, Sue Kohn, Elli Wohlgelernter, Jonathan and Ruchy Mark, Sara Barris, Nechama Kessler, and my co-author, precious friend and soul sister, Yitta Halberstam.

—Judith Leventhal

About the Authors

YITTA HALBERSTAM and JUDITH LEVENTHAL are the best selling authors of *Small Miracles*, *Small Miracles II*, and *Small Miracles of Love & Friendship*. They have both experienced an inordinate number of coincidences firsthand. Ms. Halberstam is a writer and lecturer on spirituality, whose work has appeared in many magazines, including *Parade*, *New York*, *Money*, and *Working Woman*. Ms. Leventhal is a Gestalt therapist. Both authors live in Brooklyn, New York.

❧ Believe in Small Miracles! ❧

NATIONAL BESTSELLER

Small Miracles

*Extraordinary Coincidences
from Everyday Life*

Yitta Halberstam & Judith Leventhal
Preface by Dr. Bernie Siegel, author of *Love, Medicine and Miracles*

Trade paperback, $9.95,
ISBN: 1-55850-646-2

Have you ever experienced a moment when a seemingly random event also seemed strangely meaningful, or even miraculous? *Small Miracles* is a collection of over sixty stories of such remarkable coincidences. These moving and inspirational stories—often containing profound teachings, important moral lessons, and even divine messages—will draw you out of the ordinariness of everyday life.

"A book that you'll love and cherish for a long time to come. It will make you aware of similar events that are happening to you—those touches of grace that, when we think to look for them, bless us all."

—*Belle* magazine

Available Wherever Books Are Sold

**For more information, or to order, call 800-872-5627
or visit www.adamsmedia.com**

Adams Media Corporation, 260 Center Street, Holbrook, MA 02343

Even more Small Miracles!

Trade paperback, $9.95,
ISBN: 1-58062-180-5

Trade paperback, $9.95,
ISBN: 1-55850-646-2

Trade paperback, $9.95,
ISBN: 1-58062-047-7

Three collections of true stories of remarkable coincidences that have changed the lives of ordinary people. These stories, both heart-warming and awe-inspiring, convey that coincidences are more than just random happenings—in fact, they are nothing less than divine messages.

"Judith Leventhal and Yitta Halberstam amaze and inspire with their incredible-but-true story collections . . ."

—*People Magazine*

Available Wherever Books Are Sold

**For more information, or to order, call 800-872-5627
or visit www.adamsmedia.com**

Adams Media Corporation, 260 Center Street, Holbrook, MA 02343

Have you experienced a remarkable coincidence you want to share?

If so, we would like to hear from you!

ﾟ

Send an E-mail to

storysubmissions@adamsmedia.com

Have you ever experienced an unusual, inspirational, or mysterious coincidence? We would like to hear about these personal events and possibly use them in an upcoming book. You may also mail them to:

Story Submissions
Adams Media Corporation
260 Center Street
Holbrook, Massachusetts 02343

ﾟ

All submissions will become the property of Adams Media Corporation.